DEDICATION

This book is dedicated to my friend Amanda Wright. I pray my vulnerability and courage to share my story inspires you to do the same. We did not just survive abuse, but we overcame! I thank God for healing and freedom. I love you dearly my friend.

SPIRITUALLY ABUSED & BROKEN

FROM TRAUMA TO HEALING

Sandra Pierre

Copyright © 2020 by **Sandra Pierre**

Spiritually Abused and Broken. From Trauma to Healing

All rights reserved. No part of this publication may be reproduced, distributed or transmitted in any form or by any means, including photocopying, recording, or other electronic or mechanical methods, without the prior written permission of the publisher, except in the case of brief quotations embodied in critical reviews and certain other noncommercial uses permitted by copyright law.

Although the author and publisher have made every effort to ensure that the information in this book was correct at press time, the author and publisher do not assume and hereby disclaim any liability to any party for any loss, damage, or disruption caused by errors or omissions, whether such errors or omissions result from negligence, accident, or any other cause.

Adherence to all applicable laws and regulations, including international, federal, state and local governing professional licensing, business practices, advertising, and all other aspects of doing business in the US, Canada or any other jurisdiction is the sole responsibility of the reader and consumer.

Neither the author nor the publisher assumes any responsibility or liability whatsoever on behalf of the consumer or reader of this material. Any perceived slight of any individual or organization is purely unintentional.

The resources in this book are provided for informational purposes only and should not be used to replace the specialized training and professional judgment of a health care or mental health care professional.

Neither the author nor the publisher can be held responsible for the use of the information provided within this book. Please always consult a trained professional before making any decision regarding treatment of yourself or others.

Scripture quotations are taken from the Holy Bible, New Living Translation, copyright ©1996, 2004, 2007, 2013, 2015 by Tyndale House Foundation. Used by permission of Tyndale House Publishers, Inc., Carol Stream, Illinois 60188. All rights reserved.

Scripture taken from the ESV® Bible (The Holy Bible, English Standard Version®), copyright © 2001 by Crossway, a publishing ministry of Good News Publishers. Used by permission. All rights reserved.

Cover Design by 100Covers.com
Interior Design by FormattedBooks.com
Edits by cultivatethewriter.com

ISBN 978-1-7350118-0-6 (paperback)
ISBN 978-1-7350118-1-3 (MOBI)
ISBN 978-1-7350118-2-0 (ePub)

CONTENTS

Introduction I
Part I Abuse 1
    1. Fed Up 3
    2. Church 5
    3. Illusions of Acceptance 9
    4. Danger in the Pulpit 16
    5. In too Deep 22
    6. Servant or Slave? 27
    7. Isolation 34
    8. Manipulation 42
    9. Degraded 52
    10. Exposed 59
    11. Who's your God? 65
    12. Danger 69
    13. God Intervenes 81
Part II Restoration 91
    1. Forgiveness and Healing 93
    2. It's not about me 98
    3. The Messenger 104
    4. Inside Job 114

Part III Awareness 121
    1. Can you relate? 123
    2. Friends and Family....................................128
    3. Don't be deceived.....................................132
    4. Q&A..135
Acknowledgements..143

INTRODUCTION

When you walk into a church, you typically expect to have a positive experience, but what if that wasn't the case? Could you imagine looking for answers only to find yourself confused? Can a place where you expect healing cause trauma? Well, my answer to these questions are yes and yes!

As a survivor of spiritual abuse, I will show, through my direct, unfiltered experience, that freedom and healing are possible. While every abuse case is unique, the manipulative tactics of an abuser are unmasked in the pages of this book. Testimonials by close friends and family will help you identify the signs of abuse so that you will never miss a red flag. I will also share the do's and don'ts to keep safe mentally and physically.

January 28, 2016 is a date that I will never forget. The decision to walk away from an abusive organization altered my life as I knew it. I let the fear of judgement and shame cripple my ability to speak out about the abuse. The thought of telling a stranger my story was frightening. Little did I know, two years later a 256-page book would wrestle with every fear that I had.

I flipped through the pages of a book on spiritual abuse. At the turn of every page, my hands trembled, and my heart raced. My emotions were being exposed line by line. In that moment, I didn't realize the physical symptoms were triggered by the horrific memories of abuse. I convinced myself that my ordeal was surreal, but with every account of abuse I read, reality set in. What I went through wasn't uncommon at all. That realization sparked a thought. How many people, like me, believed their situation was isolated? Consciously remaining silent while others suffered was no longer an option for me.

To the person who has been victimized, my prayer is that you will be encouraged and strengthened through my story. You might also be the person who didn't realize you are or were being abused. I would like to encourage you to know that everything you've experienced is not in vain. As you join me on this journey from trauma to healing, you will see the restorative power of God. I walk in complete freedom, and so can you!

PART I
ABUSE

1. FED UP

"All you're good for is sex! I can get that anywhere! What kind of Wife will you be! What kind of mother will you be! You're no good to me!" My fatigued body could no longer sit at the edge of the bed, listening, as Wes explicitly verbalized his feelings towards me. Each word felt like a knife violently piercing my heart. In pure anguish of a respiratory infection, I mustered enough strength to whisper two words, "I'm done." I could no longer pretend that Wes was my "happily ever after." He swept me off my feet with his gentleness, only to leave me feeling swept under a rug like dirt. The relationship I fought so hard to keep finally knocked me out emotionally.

I was afraid of change, so I found comfort in dating men who reminded me of my ex-husband. I became the girl who was a "great friend" with benefits but never good enough for a commitment. On the rare occasion a guy wanted a commitment, I thought he was crazy or someone I couldn't trust wholeheartedly.

I didn't take time to truly discover who I was and had an insatiable desire to find "the one" and live happily ever after. If it didn't work with one guy, I had a pity party then moved on to the next one. I searched, pursued, and desired companionship to fill a void, only to realize it was a God size vacancy. These men were not just fillers; they became idols. I was broken and navigating through life aimlessly.

Wes threw the key to the apartment on my bed and silently walked away. Uncontrollable tears ran down my face at the thought of another failed relationship. In desperation, I cried out to God, begging for help.

2. CHURCH

What did it look like to seek God? I spent years ignoring Him to live life my way. God wasn't pleased with my lifestyle, and I knew it. I was failing on my own and felt far away from His reach. I grew up in a single parent household where my mother was an occasional church goer. On the other hand, my father practically lived in church. I was what some would call a pew warmer. I viewed services as my time to get a feel-good message and keep it moving. However, I remembered that both my parents went to church in the good or bad times. It only made sense to seek out a community of believers during this time.

My search for a church began from the filter of feeling hopeless and rejected. I wanted a transformation. I stood in the bathroom stall after work one day, closed my eyes, and asked God to direct me to the right church. Instantly, I thought of a coworker named Lori who mentioned attending a great Bible study. I reached out to her for the address and learned the location was less than five minutes away. So, I grabbed my purse and drove directly to the address.

I pulled up to a grey commercial building that did not look like a traditional church. In a room with dim lights, soft instrumentals played, and a few people were seated with their heads bowed. A pleasant usher sat me close to the front of the stage. Though I was uncomfortable, I thought it would be rude to move farther back. An Indian guy took the stage shortly after I was settled, which was a bit different for me. I usually attended churches where everyone pretty much looked like me. In this small, intimate setting of 10, I was surrounded by a diverse group of people: Asians, Caucasians, Indians, and African Americans. I was interested to see what the interaction and service would look like.

My midweek Bible study experience was usually a mini Sunday service with less people and shorter time. So, I was surprised when the Pastor encouraged everyone to ask questions. Since I desired to learn more about God, the question and answer approach validated my need for a smaller church. After the service, Lori introduced me to the Pastor and his wife. They seemed nice, so I decided to come back the following week. Meanwhile, I continued to visit other ministries.

I was warned by my good friend Mia about attending too many churches. I thought what could possibly go wrong, church was church. On Wednesday nights, I attended The Worship Center. The ministry my coworker Lori invited me to, led by Pastor Dev. On Thursday evenings, I attended a Bible study at another church, but I couldn't decide which one to join.

Coincidently, at the Wednesday Bible study, Pastor Dev addressed visiting other churches. *"If you have a church, there is no reason that you would need to visit other churches. Your church home is all you need,"* he said. As I listened intently, I wondered if the message was for me. Pastor Dev continued, *"The person who preaches the gospel should live by the gospel. A pastor who works outside the church can't effectively minister the Word of God."* Pastor Dev explained that he spent at least 4 hours reading his Bible each day. He was speaking to me. I was attending two churches, and the Pastor at the other church had a fulltime job. I thought his message was a sign from God that I wasn't supposed to attend the other church anymore. Since I never told Pastor Dev I was visiting other ministries, I believed God was speaking through him. He assured us that we were in capable hands.

I stopped going to the other church and only attended The Worship Center. Little did I know the entire Bible study was the beginning of Pastor Dev's manipulation. It completely slipped my mind that Lori mentioned our visit to another church during a conversation with him. Pastor Dev leveraged what he knew and used his platform to sway my decision to join the ministry.

Initially, I was excited about my choice to be a member of the church. I listened to Pastor Dev share his testimony. He said God told him to leave India. We were led to believe that he gave away everything he owned in obedience to God and left his wife because she didn't want to come to the United States. He thought he would never see her again. He started his journey in the U.S. with two suitcases and nowhere to stay. Now, he lives in a 4-bedroom house with his wife who joined him in America, their beautiful daughter, and two cars.

Pastor Dev was a personable, charismatic preacher who had a persuasive way of drawing people in. I never met anyone who talked about God with such reverence. When he shared his visions, everyone wanted to be a part. Pastor Dev described the miracles he saw in India, sharing how God used him to heal the sick and even raise someone from the dead. He said casting out devils was normal, everyday occurrences for him. I was excited to have a leader who did such exploits in the name of God. I thought if God could do all this for one man, my life could surely be better if I followed Pastor Devs instructions.

3. ILLUSIONS OF ACCEPTANCE

Pastor Dev was tough on those who served in his ministry. He demanded excellence in every service. His leadership team attentively focused on everything around them, and they had a militant like demeanor when the pastor was around. If I hadn't met him prior to a Sunday service, my first impression would be that he wasn't approachable. Pastor Dev walked into church looking around, praying, and occasionally gesturing his leaders to tend to something. He didn't hide his stern approach.

During worship rehearsal, if the drummer played incorrectly or the technician didn't adjust the sound to his liking, Pastor Dev corrected them in a harsh tone. I thought, *Man, this Pastor is tough*. I wanted him to be tough on me as well. I felt I needed to be part of the "bootcamp" for my life to get on track spiritually. You see, I was the child told not to touch the hot stove but did it anyway to see what would happen. I wanted to change that and just follow instructions.

As time went on, I lingered after service and asked if I could help with anything. However, the ministry team always told me that everything was taken care of and I was free to go. Their reaction seemed odd. Out of curiosity, I asked Pastor Dev why the ministry team always declined my help. He didn't answer the question directly but said I was free to help with the cleaning and setup. My initial tasks consisted of cleaning bathrooms, classrooms, and a diaper station. I knew it was a test, but it didn't bother me. I cleaned my bathroom at home, so it wouldn't be any different at church. After a few weeks, my responsibilities increased. I was happy about helping my church because it gave me a sense of belonging.

I went from lingering around to serving and eventually spending a lot of time in church. After a Wednesday evening Bible study, I stayed later than usual as the team worked on bookstore inventory. I was interested in the various topics, so I walked around and read book summaries as the team worked. Out of nowhere, I started to feel uncomfortable. I felt like I was trying hard to fit in and should go home but, I dismissed the thought, thinking I was crazy. Mentally, I was in the best place; the clubs were no longer desirable, calling an ex wasn't a thought, and I didn't feel lonely. Why would I think I didn't belong? I was determined to progress and not self-sabotage. I wanted to be like those around me, committed and disciplined.

Ariel is the pleasant usher who greeted me during my first visit at the church. She was involved in everything. She played the drums, set up before church, volunteered as a youth leader, outreach leader, church's main point of contact, caretaker for the pastor's child, and so much more. I admired her work ethic. She was the Pastor's "right hand." I thought her being that close was cool because she learned so much. The Pastor constantly raved about Ariel's transformation after meeting him. He could see my admiration and asked if I wanted to be like Ariel; I responded yes. I wanted to experience change just like she did. I thought being involved like her and receiving correction by the Pastor would really whip me into shape.

I perceived correction as telling me when I was wrong and what needed to change. I didn't realize saying yes was an invitation for abuse to come. As much as I admired Ariel and grew closer to the team, I couldn't help but notice everyone answered questions and spoke the same way. Conversations seemed rehearsed and scripted. Aside from Pastor Dev and his wife, everyone communicated through nonverbal cues. If I asked questions or told a joke, the Pastor responded, but everyone else just smiled and made eye contact. I noticed Pastor Dev's assistant Tim wouldn't even interact with others. He either fixed something or sat in a corner on his laptop. I convinced myself that, yet again, I was overthinking and judging people I barely knew.

The nagging feeling that I didn't fit in popped up again. Although the church welcomed me, I couldn't get rid of what I felt. Instead of socializing, I decided to start leaving directly after service. A week into me rushing to leave church, Pastor Dev approached me and asked if I was okay. I shared that I was trying too hard and that he and the ministry leadership didn't care for me to be around. He told me I was like a little sister, and they all cared for me, so he would help me.

I stopped thinking about feeling rejected and started being around the ministry leadership more often. I noticed Lori didn't spend as much time as I did in church, but I was happy to be a part of the "in crowd." At work, Lori and I talked a lot about the sermons and how much we enjoyed the ministry. We had a tight bond but the more I hung out with the ministry team our friendship started to change. I had a desire to prove that I was worthy enough to be part of their circle. Truth is, there was a little girl inside of me craving the acceptance of those around her.

My first invite to hang out with the ministry team outside of church was unexpected but thrilling at the same time. I received a call from Ariel, telling me that Pastor Dev invited me to a Christmas dinner at another member's house. I happily accepted the invitation and couldn't wait to hang out with Pastor Dev's family and the rest of the ministry leaders. Unfortunately, the night before the dinner, I helped cater an event until 2:00am. The next day, I could barely get out of bed. Lori was attending the Christmas dinner so I called her that afternoon to let everyone know I wouldn't be there. We laughed as I joked about her bringing me a plate of food. I ended the call by telling Lori that Pastor Dev might get upset because I cancelled.

"Be careful what you say about a man of God. Some people walk around saying that the man of God is mean. Speaking against a man of God is not pleasing to God." I sat in the crowd listening intently to Pastor Dev's Sunday message. *Was God trying to tell me I was wrong for saying the Pastor might get upset because I cancelled?* I suddenly felt an overwhelming feeling of guilt. After service, I approached the Pastor with tears in my eyes. I apologized for not attending the dinner and said that I should have been there. I was not bold enough to tell him that I jokingly told Lori that he would be mad. I assumed it was God convicting me not to joke about anything regarding a Pastor. With a smile on his face, Pastor

Dev hugged me and said it was okay. In hindsight, his response to my apology should have been a red flag that something was wrong. He didn't even question why I was in tears about declining an invitation. I didn't know Lori told Pastor Dev our conversation word for word. He took offense to my joke and used his platform to manipulate me into condemnation. I was the perfect prey, vulnerable and desperate.

Five months into being a consistent part of the ministry, Pastor Dev called me into a meeting. I walked into a room with board members, Pastor Dev, his wife Mrs. Leita, and three other members. Before he spoke, I heard a loud instrumental sound playing in the sanctuary. Pastor Dev started the meeting by thanking everyone in the room for staying after service to speak with him. The agenda for the meeting was to discuss an issue with a ministry leader. Jenna, the leader in question, was in the sanctuary directly across from the meeting room. Hence, the reason for the loud music in the background. Jenna requested time off from ministry work to spend time with her friends and family instead of being at church all the time. Pastor Dev asked would I take her place and help with the youth Sunday school. He told me Jenna demanded her role back when she learned I was a potential replacement. I wasn't surprised at her reaction because we barely spoke. He only shared Jenna's disdain to amplify my desire to be a part of his ministry team. It worked because I agreed to take her spot. They trusted me enough to give me a leadership role.

The meeting lasted over four hours. The invitation to serve the youth led Pastor Dev to share the reason for Jenna's awkward silence during service and social gatherings. He explained when his wife was eight months pregnant, Jenna told the ministry leaders that she believed Pastor Dev liked her. When asked what gave her that impression, she explained his stares during service, him telling her how beautiful she was, and the way he hugged her were proof that he liked her. Jenna was instructed to stay silent to preserve Pastor Dev's reputation.

The discussion took an unexpected turn as each person in the room talked about Pastor Dev's character and influence. His authority carried so much weight amongst the leaders. He encouraged everyone, including me, to be the eyes and ears of the ministry. He said he needed us to uphold the vision God gave him. His words sparked the thought of a recent conversation I had with my coworker Lori. Though I was hesitant to share, my pastor just told me he trusted me with the vision God gave him. Reluctantly, I raised my hand. When all eyes shifted towards me, I expressed concerns about Lori.

I told the group that Lori felt the Pastor's opinion and spiritual guidance weren't always right. As the words flowed out of my mouth, I knew I had made a mistake. What was I doing? Lori trusted me. The guilt was written all over my face. To ease the shame, I quickly mentioned she said that we are all human and make mistakes. However, the damage was already done, and everyone in the room went radio silent. The only person unbothered in the room was Pastor Dev. My discomfort was apparent because he told me not to worry about Lori. According to Pastor Dev, she was pushing her agenda to start a church.

At 2:00 am, I finally walked out the meeting, trying to process everything that just happened. As I drove home, I thought I did the right thing concerning my coworker and was part of the team now. The illusion of acceptance clouded my judgement. Unfortunately, I had no idea the trouble I started with the simple raising of my hand that night.

4. DANGER IN THE PULPIT

The usual Bible study crew consisted of 12 people, board members, the leadership team, a few other members, and the Pastors family. We waited patiently for service to start. It was the first Bible study since the late-night meeting about Jenna and Lori. Typically, Lori arrived at church before I did. There was always a seat saved for me next to her but that day I sat on the opposite side of the sanctuary. The puzzled look on Lori's face was evidence she knew something was wrong. My demeanor towards her changed. I even avoided small talk at work. Although I was told not to worry about her, avoiding the person who invited me to the church seemed harsh. Whenever Lori walked into a room, the space felt small. The situation caused paranoia, but I shook off my concerns to focus on the teaching for that night.

After what seemed like forever waiting, service began. Pastor Dev asked us to turn our Bibles to 2 Kings 2:23-24 (All scripture was read from the King James version of the Bible, but for the sake of congruity and understanding, I am using the New Living Translation version.) Then, he read aloud, *"Verse 23,* ***Elisha left Jericho and went up to Bethel. As he was walking along the road, a group of boys from the town began mocking*** *and making fun of him. 'Go away, baldy!' they chanted. 'Go away, baldy!'* Verse 24, **Elisha turned around and looked at them, and he cursed them in the name of the Lord. Then two bears came out of the woods and mauled forty-two of them.** If I could disappear, that was the moment to do so.

With a straight face, Pastor Dev started his message for the night. He said, *"People think that it's okay to talk about a man of God. Look what happened to the kids who made fun of Elisha. How dare people walk around and say that a man of God is only human and makes mistakes. Do you know that they are anointed by God? That man of God has the authority to curse you if they choose. The Bible says touch not mine anointing."* I felt Lori's stare burning a hole through me from across the sanctuary, but I refused to look in her direction. I couldn't believe what was happening. The Pastor specifically used the words "only human" and "makes mistakes," which were Lori's words verbatim. I was mortified. Once Bible study ended, I watched Lori run out of the building. It wasn't like her to leave without speaking to everyone.

The last member couldn't leave the church quick enough for me. As I locked the church doors, I blurted out, "She knows it was me!" to the leaders who were left in the church. The ministry team nodded their heads in agreement, but Pastor Dev nonchalantly shrugged his shoulders and told me not to worry about it.

As I drove home, thoughts of worry and anxiety consumed me. *How was I going to face Lori in the office?* Pastor Dev put me in a difficult predicament. In mid thought, my phone rung. It was Lori. When I answered the phone, she didn't waste time asking if I said anything to Pastor Dev about our conversation. Though it was the moment to be honest, I lied and said no. Lori then shared that she was going to get Mrs. Leita a pair of Coach shoes, but the Pastor told her she didn't have to buy anything because his wife doesn't wear the brand. Again, I lied and told her I had no idea why he would say such a thing. The truth was Pastor Dev didn't like Lori because he felt she was planning to start a church. But, my stomach was in knots after I hung up the phone.

Immediately, I called Ariel and told her I needed to speak to Pastor Dev as soon as possible. I had to call Ariel because she was Pastor Dev's main point of contact. When he called me back, I told him about the conversation with Lori. Pastor Dev said, *"If she asks again just tell her you don't know what she's was talking about. Be wise like a serpent and gentle as a dove. She operates in witchcraft and you need to stay away from her. I believe that she's the cause of my wife's recent miscarriage."* His warning freaked me out!

I was on pins and needles at church and work. All I could think about was my Pastor telling me that Lori was a witch. I never heard anything like that in my life. To me, witches were fake people on TV, but I didn't have reason to believe Pastor Dev would lie to me. Every morning, I sped past Lori's office. The silence on both ends screamed avoidance. We went from a beautiful journey of learning about God and getting involved in church together to barely looking at each other. I was afraid to be near her. At church, the ministry team avoided her at all cost. If anyone did have to speak with her the conversations were brief and superficial. Lori didn't seem bothered at all.

A month later Pastor Dev announced to the ministry team he wanted to give Lori a chance to get back into his "good grace." His first attempt was an invitation to his daughter's birthday party. All the leaders were instructed to ignore Lori, essentially treating her like an outcast.

Everything was chaotic the day of the event. We were behind schedule with the setup. Once Lori arrived, the entire atmosphere changed. The leaders intentionally avoided walking near her; when she asked to help, everyone said no. I saw her sitting alone, which broke my heart. The few times I tried to be nice, rightfully so, she was not receptive. Based on her reaction, I figured Pastor Dev was right about Lori being a witch, so I should be obedient and stay away from her.

Though Lori had every right to be standoffish, her reaction didn't sit well with Pastor Dev. During the event He told us that she may have been chanting under her breath. We were under strict orders to not go near her at all. I questioned if what he said was true, but I was afraid to ask because I didn't want them to know I had doubts.

The guests had no idea what took place behind the scenes. Despite the madness, we all enjoyed ourselves except Lori. I thought that she surely was done with The Worship Center, but I was wrong. Lori walked into the building the following week as if nothing happened. Pastor Dev asked to speak to her privately after service. He told us Lori was no longer welcomed to attend Bible study. Pastor Dev explained to us that Lori was influencing the church members negatively, and he had to protect his sheep (church members).

The following week, we were all on high alert waiting to see if Lori would come to church. Surprisingly, she arrived bright and early with her entire family. That Sunday happened to be her birthday, and it was a normal part of our service to celebrate a member's birthday. However, Pastor Dev intentionally did not acknowledge Lori's birthday. That Sunday was the last time I saw Lori and her family at The Worship Center.

Sadly, I saw no wrong in what we did. I thought Pastor Dev was looking out for us by causing Lori to leave. To further justify our actions, Pastor Dev gave us Bible references to assure us that what we did was fine. He taught us from 1 Corinthians 5:1-13 that it was okay to remove people from the church, especially if they were influencing the congregation negatively. I accepted the teaching because it soothed all thoughts of doubt and guilt I had.

Less than two weeks of Lori leaving church my job went through a restructuring. I was relieved because Lori and I were no longer in the same department. We were on completely opposite ends of the building and never had to cross paths. I thought it was an answered prayer that I wouldn't have to see her anymore. Unfortunately, I was oblivious to the unhealthy relationship I had created with this new group of people.

Only God knows the type of hurt I caused Lori. To make matters worse, when Pastor Dev knew Lori wasn't returning to the church, he shared her personal business with the ministry team. Soon after Lori's departure, including a member's personal issues in a sermon became the norm at The Worship Center. I found myself trying to decipher who the message was about that week instead of learning the word of God. I was quickly changing for the worse.

5. IN TOO DEEP

Community Outreach and working with the youth became a big part of my life a year after joining the ministry. Volunteer work gave me a sense of purpose. As a church, we went into neighboring communities passing out flyers and praying for people. Initially, talking to strangers caused the most nerve-wracking thoughts, but the more I did it, the easier it became. I found it rewarding to touch the lives of those we reached. My zeal to do more increased daily. I wanted each person I met to find the same joy and purpose I discovered after joining The Worship Center. I felt like God was pleased with me for reaching people who didn't know Him. Rain or shine, I was excited to serve at my church every week. The issues of Pastor Devs' approach and the change in me unfolding seemed minute compared to my overall experience. I was happy and felt life had meaning.

Church events, setups, and planning took up much of my time. I joked regularly that I stayed at church longer than I did at clubs and parties. There always seemed to be something to do at church. We decorated for the change of seasons and holiday events. On those occasions, the ministry team was at church every night after work. We typically left around midnight or when the task was complete. Sundays we had two services, so I was there from 8:30 am until about midnight. Wednesdays, after Bible study we stayed late cleaning up and waiting for Pastor Dev and his family to leave. I learned that the wait was an expectation.

One night, Pastor Dev said whoever wanted to leave could go home for the night once the church was set up and our cleaning was done. I was the first one to leave then everyone followed. The next day, Pastor Dev met with the ministry leadership, excluding two older board members. He looked at me and said cuttingly, *"How dare you leave early. You should never be the first to leave the church!"* I was confused because he specifically said if we wanted to leave and get some rest, we were more than welcome to leave.

Though I didn't understand why I was being yelled at, I knew better than to question him, so I meekly said "okay." Pastor Dev proceeded to tell me that I wasn't tuned into the way he operates. The option to leave was for the two older board members in their 70s; he made it clear that we were there to serve. He explained that we left him hanging while he needed to prepare for Sunday's sermon and his pregnant wife was having a difficult time managing his young daughter. Once again, I left feeling like I did not honor my Pastor as I should. The tone was set, unless Pastor Dev or his wife were leaving the church, the leaders had to wait. He never said we couldn't leave, but it was understood that there would be consequences if we tried.

The ministry leadership consisted of three men and six women. Those numbers included Pastor Dev and his wife Mrs. Leita. We were at the church so regularly that days and nights slowly started to merge. The sun would literally set and rise while we worked at the church. The lack of people was never an excuse for something not to get done. Despite only having a team of seven leaders, everything we did had to be executed in excellence. Pastor Dev constantly thought of ways to bring people into the church, so we worked as hard as we could to support the vision.

Within a year, late nights were no longer fun for me; they increasingly became a struggle. I used to think, *Man, these people can really hang.* I noticed no one seemed bothered like me, so I did my best to keep pushing. I could not relate and ask the others how they were able to tough out the long nights. When I started to voice how exhausted I felt during our late nights at church, Pastor Dev told me that I was just lazy and didn't want to work. He emphasized that all a person needed was four hours of sleep. "*Kill your flesh*" was Pastor Dev's response to almost every concern I had. Since I wanted to serve, I pushed beyond what I felt.

Over a three-year span of being at The Worship Center, we moved into a bigger property each year. When we made the first move, the nine-person ministry team was the moving crew. Pastor Dev did the planning, told us what to move, and where to move it. He rarely helped with workload unless the items were visibly impossible to lift on our own. We had two large rooms to empty. The first room was the main sanctuary with chairs and equipment. The second room involved lifting professionally installed carpet and any ceiling fixtures.

I could never say I was tired. I had so much anxiety deciding when to take breaks and questioned whether I was being lazy. When Pastor Dev entered a room, everyone found something to do, regardless of the time. His yelling intimidated everyone. I felt like he was being a taskmaster, but I was too afraid to say anything.

Pastor Dev changed. As time progressed, cruelty replaced sternness, and anger overpowered kindness. After outreach one evening, the usual 4-member team, Ariel, Jenna, Tim, and I were headed home for the night. Since we all drove in separate cars, I asked Tim, the Pastor's assistant to stop by the church so we could grab a few things needed for an upcoming fundraiser. When I got home, I received a call from Pastor Dev. The first words I heard were, *"Are you some type of whore?* I froze as he kept yelling. *"Are you some type of Bitch? Who told you to ask [Tim] to open the church doors? Why would you ask him when I've given the usher (*who is a woman*) keys to the church?* As tears rolled down my eyes, I exhaled quickly and responded. *[Tim] was with us so I didn't think it was a problem*. I choked back tears with every word I spoke. I could hear the satisfaction in his voice. *"Don't do it again!" How was outreach?* In the same breath he cursed me out and asked about outreach. I was at a loss for words. Pastor Dev repeated his question. After responding It was okay, he hung up the phone.

Though I was shocked the Pastor spoke to me in such a degrading manner, the outward expression of his verbal abuse was imbedded in my mind subconsciously. In other words, I was already brain washed and mostly desensitized to his harsh use of language and tone. In fact, one of the first messages I heard from Pastor Dev was that people in America took curse words too seriously. He explained that words like "s**t" and "f**k" meant nothing in Indian culture. According to him, people said the word "s**t" in the pulpit all the time. As I looked around the church when he said this, some people laughed while others remained silent.

Profanity was a normal part of our conversations with Pastor Dev after his message. He made sure to use profanity in front of the leaders only, never while church members were around.

Unsurprisingly, no one questioned him. We feared him. I even said a cuss word here and there, but I knew my limit. On the other hand, Pastor Dev used his profanity disclaimer as a license to freely say what he pleased.

So, the cursing didn't surprise me the evening Pastor Dev called me. The shock was the profanity directed towards me! I thought I was in a dream. I silenced my discernment and rationalized my negative perception of Pastor Devs' words with the thoughts, *it's just your flesh; those words mean nothing*. I fought back the sting of his words and chopped it up to cultural differences. I didn't realize my silence was ammunition for continued abuse. Since I passed taking his verbal abuse test, Pastor Dev was ready to see how much further he could go.

One day the team had a late start on the service setup, so no one noticed when a new visitor entered the sanctuary. I walked out of the restroom and became startled by Pastor Dev standing in front of me. When I smiled and greeted him with a "Hello," he swiftly raised his left hand in a swinging motion as if he was about to slap me and sternly said, *"Where the f**k were you!"* When I tried to respond, he told me to get out of his face. I walked away thinking, *I wish he did put his hands on me; this would be my last day*. I was convinced that God would reveal my thoughts to him, so I quickly walked away and kept replaying in my mind, *this is a man of God. He's my Pastor, and that he only had my best interest at heart*. I repeated his favorite motto *"The boss is always right; God would bless my obedience."*

6. SERVANT OR SLAVE?

    I didn't have time to sit and think about the way I was being treated. Whether I felt anger or sadness, I pushed aside my emotions to focus on correcting my mistakes and keep working for God. On top of the weekly outreach, we planned for our Easter service, summer events, fall festival, Christmas events, summer camp, and an academy that was added to the mix. These events weren't small and required a lot of preparation; we cooked food, choreographed dances, decorated, put in extra hours for outreach on weekends, and called people to remind them about the events. All this work was being completed primarily by seven individuals: two men and five women. While Pastor Dev and Mrs. Leita planned, the seven of us focused on execution. Occasionally, church members helped, but as the ministry leadership team, it was our obligation, and we had no formal training. Most of the tasks took place after we worked our full-time jobs.

    Mrs. Leita and Tim were the brains behind the church's summer camp. They put in a lot of hours of planning while Pastor Dev oversaw it all. Expectations weren't clear to the team, and instructions changed daily. I often felt like a child getting in trouble for everything. Though we worked side by side with Mrs. Leita, she rarely told us directly when something was wrong. So, Pastor

Dev randomly yelled at us about something we had no idea we were doing incorrectly. The couple often played good cop/bad cop. Mrs. Leita tried to get his attention the moment she felt his yelling was out of hand, but it didn't stop him. I walked away confused in those moments because I couldn't understand why she wouldn't speak to us directly, knowing that he would overreact.

Mistakes were inevitable, and the consequences were draining. Nicole, a friend I referred to the summer camp program, enrolled her son. On a Friday pick up, Nicole signed her son out and told me that he would spend the following week with his grandmother. I informed her that I would tell Mrs. Leita not to expect him. After letting her know about Nicole's son, Mrs. Leita stared at me for a moment before saying, "okay." When Pastor Dev arrived at the church later, he called me over to where he and Mrs. Leita were sitting. *"Whose side are you on, the ministry's or your friend?"*, he asked. Hesitantly I responded, *"The ministry's side."* I didn't understand the reason for the question.

Out of nowhere, Pastor Dev got angry and yelled, *"How dare you tell [Leita] that [Collin]* (Nicole's son) *wasn't coming to summer camp. The summer camp is a business. If you choose your friends over the wellbeing of the ministry, then you will have no part in the growth of the ministry. You are a hindrance to what we are doing here."* My heart sank, and I felt like I betrayed them, but I didn't know how because policies and pricing seemed to be a secret. I didn't even know what a summer camp form looked like. If a person had a question, we were instructed to have them speak to Mrs. Leita. Months later, I learned a parent or guardian still had to pay the weekly fees whether the child attended or not. Finally, I understood why I got scolded, but I was still confused about why I had to choose the ministry or my friend.

The establishment of new programs continued to increase. When Pastor Dev talked about opening an academy, I was excited. I thought, *Wow! My degree will be used.* I graduated from Florida State University with a degree in Family and Child Sciences. Though I enjoyed working with infants and toddlers, I worked a corporate job when I graduated. Since the money was great, I lost sight of my original plan to open a childcare center. When I mentioned my passion was working with kids and majoring in child development one Sunday evening after church, Pastor Dev said he was asking God what I was there for and now knew. He explained they were planning to start an academy soon, and I could help with the process. The credentialing was vague, but I knew I met most of the requirements to run an academy. Pastor Dev asked me to enroll in the director credentials class, explaining it was purposeful to take the course. With minor hesitation, I agreed.

The moment my director credentials was awarded, Pastor Dev wanted the academy started. He pushed me out of my comfort zone to prepare for the county's approval process. The ministry team worked tirelessly by shopping, painting, and setting up classrooms. At first glance, the county inspector approved our classroom setup. The only issue was a safety concern of iron rods that held the playground's fence together. The inspector told us to fix the fence issue and reschedule within a month for reinspection.

However, that night, Pastor Dev asked the ministry team to pull up every iron rod attached to the fence. At 10:00 pm, we started pulling up the rods. We received one call that evening from Pastor Dev asking for a status update and encouraging us to finish quickly so that we could get some rest. At 6:00am the next morning, with raw hands and exhausted bodies, we had pulled every rod out of the ground. Within a few days, the academy was certified operational. Our tireless work on the growth of the academy continued. There was less focus on church and more focus on marketing. Pastor Dev told us there was a greater chance that families would join the church as we told the community about the academy.

Three months into working as the director of the academy, children were enrolling daily but I noticed stagnation in church growth. I prayed for direction on how to help. Since I worked from home, I thought I could help better direct the academy by setting up a remote office at the church. I figured being there would free up some time for Pastor Dev and Mrs. Leita to focus on the church needs. Pastor Dev thought it was a great idea. I offered to pay a portion of the internet service since I would use it for my paying job. Also, I volunteered to pay a portion of the cell phone used for academy inquires.

In theory, the idea of working remotely at the church sounded great. However, I didn't realize the amount of work I had to do, so I felt the emotional and physical toll quickly. Monday through Friday, I was up by 5:00am to open the academy at 6:30am. Depending on the day of the week, one or two other leaders assisted with setup. In between working my paid job, I enrolled new students, took payments if Mrs. Leita wasn't available, and responded to inquiries.

On paper, I was the academy director and lead Voluntary Prekindergarten teacher, but there was so much more behind those titles. I felt the work was never ending. According to Pastor Dev, I was distracted. My zeal dwindled daily due to exhaustion. I practically lived at The Worship Center. If it wasn't the academy, it was outreach or a church event. No matter how tired I was, my participation was a must; I couldn't say I needed a break, and I didn't want to be replaced. Soon after anyone showed signs of wanting a break from the ministry, isolation and silent treatments would follow. They were the typical consequences for any form of resistance. I had witnessed it with Jenna, Lori, and several others.

Though I continued working, help didn't increase. Pastor Devs' response to more work was *"to whom much is given much is required."* This was a Bible scripture he referenced daily. Whenever I complained about all the work, he constantly reminded me that I once complained of Christian life being boring. Pastor Dev had a scripture reference for any form of resistance or objection concerning work. I kept asking myself if something was wrong with me for thinking that maybe the work was too much. I felt so much guilt when Pastor Dev said that to me, *"You had no purpose when you came to this church but look at what you're doing now."* I managed to shut down the idea of giving up because I remember feeling lost when I got there. I had to believe all the work was for the church and had purpose.

I've always had a heart to help others, but I started to feel like a helpless slave instead of a willing servant. My desire to help Pastor Dev and his family no longer stemmed from love but fear. Every leader was either assigned a task or started one with the expectation that he or she would own it. Two leaders were responsible for helping the pastor's family. They were responsible for their two kids, their food, and laptop bags. I was backup if one wasn't available to help. As time passed, Tim focused solely on helping Pastor Dev while Ariel and I helped with the children.

If we weren't outside when the Pastor's car pulled into the parking lot, we would get yelled at by Pastor Dev; his yells felt like piercing daggers. I always walked away in tears or felt some type of guilt. In fact, the whole team would get yelled at because no one was exempt, so for the most part, we tried to look out for one another. If I didn't notice they arrived, someone quickly told me they were there. If I wasn't in place, my help was no longer needed. Pastor Dev boasted about the privilege we had to serve an anointed man of God. When I was in the hot seat, being told I wasn't needed made me feel rejected and useless.

The weight of serving was dreadful. With each added responsibility, I wanted to run away. His daughter Ashely was 4 years old, and his son AJ just turned a year old. The ministry team cared for the Pastors' children while they worked and preached. It was a responsibility that we did not take lightly at all. I was responsible for their son AJ while Ariel watched Ashley. I supervised, changed diapers, and fed AJ. I adored the kids but feared the responsibility. The anxiety that followed any scrape or tear of the children was overwhelming. When Pastor Dev yelled, it was so intimidating; I never could get used to it. The rage in his tone was worse than a punch in the face, at least in my mind. I didn't want the responsibility anymore. I could not effectively watch the children and remain sane. It was just too much pressure, but I had no idea how to voice what I felt. All I could hear in my head was Pastor Dev's voice, *"It's a privilege to serve an anointed man of God."*

The first invitation to my Pastors' home was not quite what I expected. Pastor Dev called me one evening to tell me that he needed Ariel, Jenna, and I to come to his house because Mrs. Leita needed our help. The welcome into their home was a short-lived honor for me. After greeting one another, we were all put to work. Their Saint Bernard had drooled all over the walls and tile; I was tasked with cleaning the walls and scraping off shedding dog hair stuck to the dried-up saliva. It took me more than three hours to complete the nauseating work, but I had to honor my leaders. Unfortunately, I did such a good job that Pastor Dev assigned me to that task whenever we were asked to help clean their home.

The dreadful "we need help" text only meant come clean. Even setting up a Christmas tree was part of our task because the Pastor didn't have time. We weren't invited to their home just to enjoy spending time as a community of believers; instead, we always worked. Though Pastor Dev always asked for our help, it was in the form of an unspoken command. His request would come after spending the day at church or a Saturday night we thought we had to ourselves. Pastor Dev told us to always make ourselves available. If we missed his call, we had to explain why. Our reasons were excuses to him. His response never changed. "God can't use a vessel that's not available," he would say. His tactics strategically led into another plan. Every conversation about being available to go to his house whenever he requested was the beginning of his plan to distance us from any outside influence.

7. ISOLATION

Availability was a tactical key to isolation. I found myself turning down invites to hang out with friends and family to ensure I was available when Pastor Dev called. The invites slowly stopped because I was always busy. The leadership joked about their family not calling because they were always in church. We didn't realize that's exactly what Pastor Dev wanted. On extended holiday weekends, such as Thanksgiving, Memorial Day, and Independence Day, he always had a plan for the ministry team to hang out. We either went to his home or somewhere out of town. We weren't forced to go, but again, invites were unspoken commands.

Vacations and hanging out at Pastor Dev's house weren't fun to me. I went because I knew saying no wasn't an option. Pastor Dev and Mrs. Leita enjoyed their break while we were responsible for caring for the kids. Relaxation was out the question. We couldn't sleep in if we wanted to. We had to do everything Pastor Dev wanted to do, and I hated it. Not only did I have to go on vacations that I wasn't thrilled about, but I had to spend money that I didn't have. If we couldn't afford the trips, Pastor Dev fronted the cost and put us on payment plans. So, I owed them money that I didn't voluntarily request. The whole arrangement was simply awful.

Many times, I just wanted to go home and relax, but Pastor Dev made me feel like being an introvert was demonic. Unfortunately, I believed him. I could not shake the desire to be by myself, so I thought something was wrong with me. I thought it was possible that I was possessed. To further his agenda of isolating us from friends and family, Pastor Dev spent significant time talking about the study of demons.

We were taught so much about demons that I walked around thinking anyone who didn't receive the same teaching I had was possessed with a devil. Pastor Dev preached the importance of the power of association and referenced Psalm 1:1 to prove his point. He told us that demonic spirits would torment us if we didn't choose the right people associations. He also assured us that being part of his ministry made us okay. Between all the work and being paranoid, I rarely spent time with anyone outside of The Worship Center. Pastor Dev told me if I focused on ministry, God would provide everything I needed; he referenced Matthew 6:33, which states, "But seek ye first the kingdom of God, and his righteousness; and all these things shall be added unto you" (KJV).

Isolation didn't stop with those outside the church. I worked with a team of people I couldn't connect with. Pastor Dev had a rule that unless he was present, we couldn't hang out with other leaders in the church. He reinforced that we should never get personal in ministry. If Pastor Dev wasn't around, everyone seemed rigid with one another. To assure we followed his rules, we unconsciously became frenemies.

Pastor Dev told Ariel I was a flirtatious girl so she should watch me closely. She believed him and stayed away. When my responsibilities increased, he started comparing strengths and weakness to keep Ariel and me in competition. If people I invited to church during outreach didn't show up, he would tell me that Ariel doesn't have that problem because she knew how to reach people. I had to push harder and do whatever she did. The comparison created friction between us. He also belittled us in front of one another. Pastor Dev constantly said Ariel was dumb and didn't have common sense. Sadly, I heard it so much that I started to believe it. I found myself annoyed with Ariel for no reason at all. He created negative perceptions among the ministry leadership team to keep the focus on him.

Jenna and I were an entirely other issue. The moment I took her role working with the youth, our relationship became non-existent. We only spoke when we had to. Ultimately, I had to work and spend time with a team of people while still feeling isolated.

When planning the first kids' fest, I had to work closely with Jenna and Ariel. Surprisingly, I saw a different side of Jenna and realized we had a lot in common. We laughed and joked as we worked with no tension at all. As we unpacked decorations, Pastor Dev walked in and went straight to the pulpit. We said hello, but he ignored us. I knew something was up. Pastor Dev played enough mental games for me to recognize that the silent treatment and lack of recognition meant I was in trouble. So, I walked up to the pulpit where he was standing. *"Did I do something wrong?",* I asked. He wasted no time with his response. *"You don't care about your spiritual life, do you? That's why demons attack you. Didn't I tell you to stay away from her? Why were you sitting next to her? You know that she likes girls, and you're sitting there smiling and laughing with her."*

I stood quietly overwhelmed with his flood of questions. *"Answer me,"* He said. Stumbling over my words I answered him with my head down, *"We were working, and she said something funny."* He sternly pointed a finger at me and discreetly spoke, *"Next time I see you sitting and laughing with her, I will not say anything else to you. I'll let you deal with those demons on your own."* I figured he didn't want Jenna to hear what he said. I assured him it wouldn't happen again.

When I moved my work to the other side of the sanctuary, it was obvious that Jenna was the topic of discussion. I felt so uncomfortable that night. I knew her feelings were hurt. I was too afraid to say anything else to her or Pastor Dev.

Pastor Dev's goal to create a form of isolation amongst the ministry team was to prevent us from sharing thoughts and feelings with one another. When relationships are formed, you share personal thoughts and views. Imagine if I told Jenna or Ariel the doubts I had, and they shared the same feelings. Agreement would remove doubt and eliminate the thought that I am overreacting. So, the focus stayed on Pastor Dev regardless of what he did. Even the books we read only came from the church bookstore. Pastor Dev told us that he read every book in the store before it was added to inventory, so they were safe books to read. He said we should stay away from other books. It was the same way with movies and the places we went. Nothing happened outside of Pastor Dev, at least not with his knowledge. At some point, he found a way to demonize anything outside of his grasp.

Our families were always the main target of isolation because they were the closest individuals to us. I had a cousin in trouble who called me and asked if I would take temporary custody of his daughter until he was released from prison. Of course, I wanted to help because he's family, but I had to decide quickly. I went to Pastor Dev and Mrs. Leita for advice on whether I should accept the duty. Pastor Dev said it was a huge responsibility to take on and I would no longer have the freedom to be involved in ministry the way I was. If I decided to take her in, that meant less ministry work. He said I couldn't just pick up and go as I wanted. I assured him that I understood the sacrifice I had to make, which wasn't the answer he expected. Then, he explained I would also have to deal with the spirits attached to the child from the mother and father. Of course, I became scared when he mentioned spirits.

Pastor Dev spent so much time discussing demons that I over spiritualized everything. He said the enemy was using this situation to creep back into my house. He reminded me that Luke 11:24-26 talked about the evil spirit coming back to a house that was swept clean and returning with seven more spirits. He said I was doing well in ministry; I'd been delivered from past hurts, and now, I was allowing someone else's mistake to mess me up again. Mrs. Leita asked why I was willing to sacrifice when the mother and father didn't care enough about their child to stay out of trouble. I felt badly, but I was afraid to take her in, so I gave my family a lame excuse about my finances not being in order to have a child in my care. The truth was Pastor Dev incited fear to keep me away from my family.

Slowly, I was cutting off everyone in my life. I hurt so many people around me. I confidently told everyone I was doing the work of the Lord and didn't have time for them. If I mentioned the lack of support from a friend or family member, Pastor Dev told me to cut them off. He told us a person who didn't support our walk with God was no friend, so that is exactly what I did. I honestly believed cutting people out of my life was a selfless act.

Mia, the friend who warned me about visiting too many churches was one of the first people I cut out my life. I felt like she didn't support me in anything concerning church. When I spoke to Pastor Dev about how I felt he told me to let her go. On her birthday, I sent her a text telling her we could no longer be friends. How devastating that must have been for her! Mia and I were glued to the hip. Her youngest child was my goddaughter. I couldn't face her in person, so I sent a text. I never got over it, but I thought I was honoring God. One person after another, I slowly lost those close to me.

I didn't realize how messed up I was from Pastor Dev's manipulation. I was brainwashed and didn't know it. The relationships dear to me kept being cut off. One relationship posed an ultimate threat to my time at The Worship Center. The person who lived in my home. It was easy for Pastor Dev to convince us to end relationships outside our home but inside the home was a different story.

My friend Wanda expressed that she was ready to leave Tallahassee. It was like a light bulb went off in my head, so I told her that she could come and stay with me. At the time, my church was looking for singers. I knew Wanda had an amazing voice. I volunteered to help her move and assumed she would join my church. I told Pastor Dev my plan. He thought she would come to the church as well, so he said it was a great idea. Her first Sunday at the service, Wanda sat towards the back of the sanctuary. When Pastor Dev entered the church, he looked at me to confirm the person sitting in the back of the room was Wanda. I walked over and made the introduction. After the service, Wanda didn't have much to say about The Worship Center. She thought it was just okay.

Wanda spent a lot of time at the apartment on her own while I was always at church. Fortunately, she had friends in the area. She only came to The Worship Center twice. I knew she didn't care to come to my church because she started attending another church. It wasn't part of the plan to have someone in my house who went to a different church. Finally, I asked for Wanda's honest opinion about The Worship Center. She simply stated it wasn't for her.

When I told Pastor Dev that Wanda decided to attend another church, he responded by telling all the leaders God showed him that she struggled with masturbation and molestation. I didn't understand why he chose to say those things in front of everyone, but I stayed silent. Later that day, I tried to convince Wanda that Pastor Dev was the real deal and she should visit again. I shared what he said God showed him about her. Wanda broke down in tears and completely shut down. We were both uncomfortable in the house. Wanda broke the silence after a few days by telling me she was moving out. She said I never took her anywhere, and all I did was go to church. I told her nothing was wrong with being in church all the time. I also explained that I felt like she was using me, so she shouldn't delay her move. The next day, I sat in my room as Wanda packed her stuff and left. Neither of us said goodbye. In a short span of 2 months seven years of friendship was destroyed.

All the loss was heart breaking. I hid my feelings because I was taught God would reward me for my obedience. My every thought was replaced by something Pastor Dev said. With every loss, he told me God would bring the right connection. Though I was on a downward spiral that I could see, if I questioned my involvement at The Worship Center, Pastor Dev would admonish me with the reminder, *"Don't take a man of God's presence lightly. The anointing of God rubs off on those who remain close."* I thought I was ungrateful for missing my family and friends, so I suffered in silence with the hopes that God would take my pain away.

8. MANIPULATION

Manipulators are always looking for the perfect prey. They skillfully evaluate their target and remove any hindrance to hunt them down. Without knowing it, I was a target the moment I walked into The Worship Center. Pastor Dev started his hunt as soon as he realized my desperation to seek God and willingness to make any change necessary. He studied me, and I passed his first test when I joined the church. Weeks later, my tearful apology for not attending a Christmas dinner was another check on his list. Check mark three occurred when I shared the words of my coworker during the leadership meeting. Finally, my lack of response to his verbal abuse was confirmation that Pastor Dev could do whatever he wanted. I couldn't see that my need for acceptance gave Pastor Dev access to a door I didn't even know existed in a church setting: the door of abuse.

I did everything Pastor Dev told me to do. If his family or ministry would benefit, there was no limit to what leadership could do, including me. It was okay to steal for the ministry. It was nothing to take a few name tags, candy for Sunday school, markers, and crayons from a store. Soon after, we began to steal for personal gain. Though I knew stealing was wrong, I feared Pastor Dev more than I feared God and the law. My moral compass went in whatever direction Pastor Dev dictated it should go.

We spent late nights working at the church. As a safety precaution, we were required to send a text message letting Pastor Dev know when we made it home. We also had to text him whenever we arrived at the church. Clearly, Pastor Dev had eyes everywhere. Essentially, each person sent a private text to him on a specific leaders' whereabouts. Pastor Dev trusted no one.

When an official group chat was established, it became a competition to see who could send the first text message informing Pastor Dev that someone arrived at the church. We all wanted to show him we were attentive and effectively managing our assigned task. If I didn't respond to his call or text, Pastor Dev sent a group text thanking the specific person who responded. It was an indirect way of making us feel badly for not answering the call. Pastor Dev intentionally ignored my return call, and I would spend the rest of the night wondering if I would get yelled at for not answering in time.

Occasionally, on Saturday morning, the academy was opened for one child. After signing out the child one afternoon, I went straight home and fell asleep. When I woke up, I had a missed call from Pastor Dev. He left a voicemail saying he knew I was sleeping, and I was a lazy, disgusting girl. Later that day, Mrs. Leita thanked Jenna in our group text for answering her phone and being available to take payment from a parent who was waiting at the church. I knew the purpose of her text was to make me feel badly for not being available. Despite knowing her intent, I felt like I was on pins and needles awaiting punishment.

The next day, while the ministry team was having lunch, Pastor Dev openly thanked Jenna for answering her phone then said God will only use someone who wants to be used. I felt uncomfortable and shame at his indirect message to me. Yet again, I had done something wrong that supposedly did not please God. I took on the notion that I was useless and couldn't be used by God. All I could do was sit in the room silently. Their manipulative tactics affected my psyche on levels I can't put into words. I felt like I was losing my mind, yet I could do nothing about it.

Outspoken members stayed on Pastor Dev's radar and typically, didn't last long. They were labeled problem members. Once a person was identified as a problem, the team had to surveillance their every move. Pastor Dev had a mother and daughter duo in the church who annoyed him. We could always count on them to speak their minds. Every ministry leader, including me, had to report their actions. We had no idea what they were capable of until it was too late. During the celebration of our new church building, the mother of the duo walked up to the stage, grabbed a microphone, and started singing a song. She worshipped and thanked God for providing a new building to have service. Though we were caught off guard, we all joined in and praised God. I looked around and saw people crying tears of joy, even Pastor Dev was crying. After the service ended, with a stern look on his face, he instructed us that the evening service was cancelled, and we'd better arrive on time because God wanted him to deal with us. Seven o'clock in the evening couldn't arrive quickly enough for me; I was a nervous wreck trying to mentally play out what was going to take place when we returned to church. I walked into a room filled with anxious leaders. Some had their heads down while others twiddled their fingers, waiting for what was to come.

Pastor Dev walked directly to the pulpit, sat down, and stared at us. Then, he calmly said, *"You were all out of order for letting [Monique] come up to the mic. None of you are operating in a spirit of excellence; [She] could see how unorganized you were and took advantage of the moment. [Monique] was out of line and you guys gave her the authority to stand on this stage."* It didn't make sense that we were being blamed for something he could have stopped. To my surprise, Pastor Dev pointed at me and said, *"And you, do you think ministry is a joke? A few weeks ago, you shared a dream that you had where you heard a voice ask you were you going to choose man or Him? God is warning you that this is your last chance. He brought you here because this is a church of last chances. Look around you. Think about how everyone of you came here hopeless and now your lives are so much better. No one here has any room to mess up. God is trying to grow you in this ministry. Sandra you are here because God favored your father's faithfulness."*

Pastor Dev's words broke me down. He knew how much my father meant to me. I talked about how hard he worked to take care of us. I shared how guilty I felt for complaining and giving my father a hard time as a child. There were no dry eyes down the row.

My expectation of praise from the Pastor diminished daily. Despite my efforts, negative criticism followed me everywhere. I spent so much time in church, but I wasn't closer to God. I couldn't figure out what was wrong with me. Every time I had a thought, it seemed as if Pastor Dev's sermons were about me. During one time of confusion, his message was about keeping a clean focus. Immediately, I felt uneasy. As he preached, I prayed to God for forgiveness. Though I worked long hours at the church, I rarely spent time in prayer or reading my Bible. Truthfully, I only opened my Bible after Pastor Dev yelled at us for not answering his question correctly. I told myself that I would do better balancing ministry and my time with God.

However, I was soon in trouble again. The silent treatment started directly after his message as Pastor Dev sat at the lunch table interacting with everyone but me. I spoke directly to him, but he acted as if I was invisible. I knew the tactic all too well. When Pastor Dev acted as if you didn't exist, it was the queue to ask him what was wrong. With a sigh, I asked Pastor Dev if I did something wrong.

He responded with a question, *"Are you distracted?"* I thought, *Yup, I knew he was talking about me in his message.* I replied, *"Not really."* He looked at me again and said, *"Are you focused?"* I said, *"For the most part, I am."* He looked agitated. *"Are you on Facebook in the office?"* My response, *"Not really"* didn't come quick enough. Unexpectedly, he yelled, *"Stop lying to me, you Bitch."* All I could do was cry. Then, Pastor Dev looked me in the eye and said, *"Don't start with those tears because that's fake and women do that to manipulate situations. Do you spend time on Facebook while working in the office?"* As tears streamed down my face, I shrugged my shoulders and told him *"sometimes."* I was praying in my head that he would just get to the point. The moment was so intense, I unconsciously kept holding my breath. *"God already showed me that you spend most of the time on Facebook trying to talk to men,"* he said. I looked over at Mrs. Leita who silently ate her lunch. God didn't show him anything about me; it was Mrs. Leita. Pastor Dev said, *"You are not focused.*

Every day we are finding mistakes in the academy paperwork." I barely had time to myself let alone time to talk to men on Facebook. Despite my innocence, I apologized to Pastor Dev. He always found a way to convince me that I was the problem.

I believed Pastor Dev knew he couldn't out right physically hit the women on the team. However, he didn't have a problem kicking and punching his assistant Tim around. Ultimately, he figured out an elusive way to do the same to me and the other women. As the point of contact at the church, I was responsible for calling church members to let them know about service updates. During an evening service, we averaged two families and the ministry leaders, so the call list wasn't long. Pastor Dev decided to cancel an evening service because his daughter wanted to go to the pool. He said we could all use the break. I was told to call the members and let them know service was cancelled for the evening. However, I wasn't allowed to share the reason; I was tasked with letting them know we were working on cleaning the "edifice" or building.

On our way to the pool, we stopped at a local store to find swimsuits for the kids and ourselves. While in the parking lot discussing what we should buy, I accidentally pocket dialed Ms. Victoria, the last member I called regarding service being cancelled. I thought the phone was locked and continued walking into the store. After service the following Sunday, Pastor Dev looked at me and said, "I'll deal with you in a minute." I had no idea what was going on.

When the last member left the church. The ministry team stood around talking about the service and trying to figure where we would eat lunch. I was too nervous to participate. Pastor Dev stopped the conversation and stared at me. Disappointedly, he said, *"I've never been in a position where I had to give answers to a member, and today you put me there."* Apparently, Ms. Victoria told him that she knew what we did on Sunday. Pastor Dev told her we were cleaning the church that day. Ms. Victoria said we were at the pool because I accidentally dialed her number, and she heard us talking about what we purchased at the store. Nikki, Ms. Victoria's daughter, told Pastor Dev that her mom listened to our entire conversation instead of hanging up the phone. He quickly walked up to me saying that he never runs out of the words, but at that moment, he was so embarrassed, and it was all my fault.

The leadership team started laughing, I was laughing, and Mrs. Leita said, *"Sandra, you deserve it today."* Then, Pastor Dev started kicking my legs repeatedly. I tried to block his kicks as I laughed off the pain. The intensity of those kicks did not feel like a playful game as he called it. I could tell that he meant to make me feel those kicks because of the force behind them. I kept a smile on my face. We were taught that "the hitting game" was the way Pastor Dev played around with his sister, so we should all be team players. I rubbed my legs as I apologized to Pastor Dev, but internally, I was livid.

I couldn't control the crying, but I learned to add laughs to show I was a team player. Once Pastor Dev got comfortable with me being around, he played punching games, and no one could question or say you didn't want to play. I can't remember how these games were introduced. It started out of nowhere during our lunches after church or when we visited his home. We never knew when the game would start. The only persons who did not get hit was Jenna and Mrs. Leita. I assumed Mrs. Leita was not included because she was his wife, but he told us Jenna was too petite and couldn't handle his games.

The punches and kicks sometimes left bruises, and I would be in tears. At the onset of the "hitting games," I initially cried or got mad. Then, Pastor Dev would ask me if I saw anyone else crying and accused me of being too sensitive or in my flesh for getting angry. The ministry team often told me to *"Toughen up Sandra. It's just a game."*

The game was a manipulative tactic. It was Pastor Dev's training ground to make hitting and punching acceptable. If I or anyone on the team said or did something he thought was wrong, Pastor Dev played the "hitting game." Ariel and I would compare our bruises as if they were normal. Randomly, Pastor Dev would tell us that in India, if a man beat his wife, the police didn't get involved. He thought it was crazy how Americans believed authorities could get in a man's family affairs. He even shared how he hit his wife when they were in India and vowed to never do it again. Though I was trained in a domestic violence shelter and worked with women who were physically and sexually abused, I couldn't see all the signs of an abuser in Pastor Dev. I was blinded by the title 'Pastor.'

Members weren't exempt from Pastor Dev's manipulation. He used and hurt anyone he could. Tina, her husband Daryl Williams, and their three kids were one of the two faithful families who showed up to every service. They showed their support and volunteered when they had time. Pastor Dev found a way to criticize them, by claiming that the Williams family was trying to imitate his life. He told the ministry team they purchased the same car that he bought for his wife. I was shocked when he stood on stage and said, *"The people in the church keep focusing on a man of God's life instead of their own. People who copy an anointed man of God won't get anywhere in life. They go out and purchase cars like me. They even try to dress like me."* I looked at Mrs. Leita, who was also caught off guard by his message. Although Pastor Dev did not mention anyone specifically, the congregation had less than 30 members on a regular Sunday. The only person who recently purchased the same car was the Williams family.

The Williams family didn't show up the following Sunday, nor did they attend Bible study. Pastor Dev told me to call them and make sure they were okay. After my multiple attempts to reach Tina and Daryl, Pastor Dev decided to call himself. Tina answered and agreed to meet with Pastor Dev a few days later. I have no idea how he corrected the issue, but the Williams family agreed to stay at the church.

The pulpit was a weapon that Pastor Dev used to manipulate, hurt, and push people out of the church. Messages that targeted individuals like the Williams family and many others were normal occurrences at The Worship Center. Pastor Dev told us whoever left the church was cursed. As a leadership team, we would sit around and gossip about the members we didn't like and point out their flaws. Though no one was forced to say anything, if Pastor Dev agreed, we were free to say what we pleased. The gossiping also became a norm. I was okay with gossiping if it was someone I didn't care for, which was wrong and selfish. The laughter and jokes about members leaving wasn't a problem to the ministry team. In fact, Pastor Dev proudly boasted about making members leave. Whenever I was on the receiving end, I was told to toughen up and get out of my flesh, so I conformed to my environment. "Toughening up" not only caused me to be insensitive to those around me, but also to myself.

9. DEGRADED

Pastor Dev's direct attacks on me wouldn't stop. He pushed constantly to see how far I would let him go with the verbal and emotional abuse. After he got tired of yelling and the silent treatments, Pastor Dev started humiliating me. I felt trapped in a mental prison with no way out.

One day, Jenna asked if I had a sanitary napkin she could have. When I told her that I only use tampons, the other ladies standing nearby laughed as they questioned why I used them. Pastor Dev, who was listening from a distance, shouted out that only loose women wore tampons. Then, he said it was ungodly for anything other than your husband's penis to enter your vagina. I was mortified, and it was apparent by my look. The other ladies walked away silently. Pastor Dev knew he hurt my feelings, but he didn't care. As I continued working, I overheard him tell his wife, *"Her flesh needs to die. Feelings are just a manifestation of an overactive flesh."*

A few months later, Pastor Dev asked me if I had feminine products. When I told him I had pads, he said, *"No, those other things."* After I shared that I stopped using tampons, Pastor Dev walked away without saying anything. Then, I overheard him tell Jenna that I didn't have any tampons. I was appalled that he asked me for the very item he condemned me for having a few weeks ago. I thought I was going crazy as I thought, *is there anything I can do, right?*

Apparently, Pastor Dev enjoyed hurting our feelings. On another day, I joked about Jenna going on a movie date. She looked at me and replied that nothing was wrong with going on a date. All the leaders laughed in agreement, except Pastor Dev; he looked intently at me while indirectly talking to Jenna and said, *"Only whores would sit in a dark theatre with a man that wasn't her husband."* Shocked, Jenna walked away in tears. Pastor Dev could tell I felt badly because of the expression on my face. He told me to, *"Let her go."* Any time someone's opinion went against what Pastor Dev felt, he made sure that person walked away from the conversation feeling ashamed.

Conversations during leadership gatherings became progressively worse. Our lunches usually involved jokes as well as talks about the service and sermons. Pastor Dev randomly started inappropriate conversations with us. On one occasion, he asked us how many sexual partners we had though our conversation had nothing to do with that subject. When no one answered, he looked at me and said, *"I know you've had a threesome and anal sex."* All eyes turned to me. I simply replied, *"No"* and held back tears. Crying was a sign of defeat, and I didn't want him to win that day but the humiliation I felt replaced my tears.

Pastor Dev instructed us to keep all sex discussion amongst the ministry team because he preferred that we talk to him instead of acting on our desires. Though Pastor Dev encouraged us to talk to him, if he deemed the conversation out of line, he tore us down with his words and called us carnal. I never knew what he expected from us because when we followed his rules, we still got in trouble.

A new family that included a young woman, her boyfriend, and their daughter started attending The Worship Center through a Friday night outreach invite. Dreya and her boyfriend Paul enjoyed the service so much that they enrolled their daughter in the center's academy. During pick up hours, Paul asked to make a payment; as he waited for his receipt, he joked about getting a discount on childcare. When I informed Pastor Dev, he told the ministry team that Paul didn't act like that with his wife, so I must have enticed him to respond that way. Though I never flirted with Paul, Pastor Dev made it seem like I did. I realized that he and his wife agreed that I had a flirtatious nature and had this conversation about me before. My silence must have indicated that I didn't agree with them because Pastor Dev started to give more examples of my "flirtatious behavior."

Allegedly, two years prior, Pastor Dev said he drove by the church and saw me flirting with an officer who was a summer camp guest speaker. He explained to the team that I gave the officer all my attention and neglected the children. I knew it was a lie, but I remained quiet though the other leaders' perception of me was tainted. The story about him driving by was bogus; Mrs. Leita had simply told him that I flirted with the officer. Pastor Dev never passed up an opportunity to humiliate me. Each time, the Pastor or his wife pointed out what they believed was a character flaw, I slowly felt that I was being reduced to nothing.

One example wasn't enough because Pastor Dev had something to prove that day. He then said his assistant complained regularly that I ran around in outreach with my chest poking out, flaunting my breasts. According to Pastor Dev, they never mentioned it to me because it eventually stopped. I was so excited about reaching people for Christ, and I was offended that Pastor Dev believed his assistant. Everything I did with a desire to please God was devalued.

    I had questions in my mind. *One, what did flirting look like driving 45 miles an hour past a store front church? Two, did he bother to consider his assistant might be a pervert? Lastly, could he just admit that his wife fed him those lies about me flirting?* Of course, I couldn't verbalize my thoughts because I would lose that battle. But, I started to question my identity. I no longer felt comfortable being me because everything about me seemed to be a problem. My voice began to diminish with every accusation. Still, I did my best to conform to what the Pastor said was right. I learned that Pastor Dev didn't have limits. He crossed every boundary he could think of. At one point, I thought suicide was my best option out of that place. Though a gun wasn't held to my head, Pastor Dev's invisible chains of fear wouldn't let me go.

    The day I found the courage to do something I wanted, it left Pastor Dev enraged. I volunteered to pick up the food orders for the ministry team. I left while Pastor Dev figured out what movie he wanted us to watch that night. After I picked up the order, my car wouldn't start, so I sent a message to the group chat letting everyone know what was going on. As I waited for AAA, Pastor Dev sent Jenna to pick up the food. When AAA arrived, they were unable to jump my car. Since I lived less than two miles away, my car was towed to my apartment. I called Ariel and asked her to give everyone an update. When Pastor

Dev called to tell me, he sent Jenna to pick me up, I told him it was okay because I caught a ride with the tow truck driver. I didn't feel like going back to the church, so I used the situation to my advantage. I felt like I gave the wrong response, but I was already home. I sent a group text thanking Jenna for leaving to pick me up and wished everyone a good night. Not one person responded. I knew Pastor Dev told them not to respond; silence always indicated that something was wrong.

A few days passed with no mention of the incident. Pastor Dev was yelling at me about something he was not happy about. He accused me of being a selfish human being and brought up the tow truck incident. He explained it was selfish of me to ride with the tow truck driver when they were sending someone to get me. I tried to explain that I was already in the tow truck when I called them.

Out of nowhere, Pastor Dev brought up my ex-husband. He said he realized my ex-husband wasn't the problem; my marriage ended because of me. He claimed my life would suck, and I would never have what God wanted me to have or be who God wanted me to be if I didn't change my ways. I would be alone for the rest of my life and no man would want to be with me. As he spoke, I heard a voice in my head say, *Kill yourself*. Once my tears subsided, I was hurt to the core. Pastor Dev laughed and said, *"You're not going home to kill yourself, right?"* I replied, "No Sir." He moved on to giving me outreach instructions. In a sarcastic tone, he asked if I would be at outreach the next day. Choking back tears, I said yes when I really wanted to say no.

I already knew Pastor Dev's mode of operation. When he wanted to prove a point, our tears were the benchmark of a job well done. I went home in so much pain, but the grace of God truly kept me that night. My heart was aching, and I felt like I had no worth. I woke up the next morning with my eyes swollen shut from crying all night. I kept telling myself that I was a failure with nothing to live for. Pastor Dev told me I was like a sister to him and his intent was to help me change and grow in the things of God. In my mind, showing up every day was proof that I could handle his "tough love."

Using racial slurs was another way that Pastor Dev belittled and humiliated us. He openly told the leaders, *"Black people with dreads and those medusa looking braids are disgusting. It doesn't matter how much they clean up; they look nasty and greasy. Blacks in India are called negros and they are usually shoe shiners."* I pointed to Ariel and Jenna and said, *"Pastor Dev, you know that we are black, right?"* He tried to clean up his comments. *"You are a Haitian and they are Jamaican. Haitians and Jamaican were not slaves."* I chuckled subtly and explained that our ancestors were slaves from Africa. I couldn't tell if it was pure ignorance or Pastor Dev was trying to deflect that I low key called him out on his racist comments. He moved on by stating, *"Your cultures are different, and you guys don't act like black Americans."* I knew my limit, so I sat quietly as he defended himself.

Pastor Dev was racist, but I couldn't be the one to tell him. He called black people who came to visit the church "niggers" while Mexicans were called "beaners." He said he preferred more whites in the church. If he sensed a slight bit of uneasiness from me, he would say, *"I see you're in your flesh."* Pastor Dev constantly reminded the ministry team that anger was a flesh issue, and he intentionally provoked us to kill our flesh. He further explained that if we were moved by words created by man, our flesh was active, and we were not being led by God. When I felt my anger rising, I told myself that it was only my flesh, and I needed to fight the feeling.

"Black people can't have straight hair. Their hair only looks like a sponge," were comments Pastor Dev used to provoke me to anger. When I straightened my hair, he looked at me in disgust and commented, *"You're not white…that doesn't look right on you."* Also, he preached that wearing braids and dreads was demonic; we were instructed to look up images of Medusa for examples of what braids looked like. During Bible study, Pastor Dev told the congregation small braids that black people wore (box braids and micro braids) carried spirits in them. He said one or two natural braids with our hair was okay but not plaits with weave. I blindly followed as Pastor Dev molded the congregation to what he deemed acceptable.

10. EXPOSED

I walked in on Pastor Dev showing Jenna pictures. He instructed me to come and look at the pictures, which were of a woman who liked him in his younger days. Without thinking, I said, "Why are you showing us pictures of another woman Pastor Dev? I don't think that's right. You're our Pastor. *If it ain't your wife, I don't want to see it.*" I don't know where I got the boldness that day, but I said it. He looked at me with disbelief and said nothing was wrong with showing a picture of a friend to us. Clearly, something was wrong because his wife left the church in tears that night.

Days later, Pastor Dev showed the ministry team the picture of the woman again. He shared that she came to Tampa looking for him, found the location of his gym, and was watching him for some time. He wanted us to know what she looked like in case she came to the church. The story didn't seem real, so I said, "*That's disrespectful; why would she come to the church?*" As Mrs. Leita agreed with me, Pastor Dev responded, "*Shut up Bitch.*" Though it was normal to hear him call us out of our name, we never heard him do it to his wife. So, we were shocked. The following day, Pastor Dev told me that I was part of his ministry team, but I did not stand by him concerning the issue of this woman. Instead of agreeing with him, Pastor Dev said I was being a

Judas. I couldn't believe my loyalty to the ministry and his family was being questioned, and I was being called a traitor.

A few weeks later I walked out of my office for a quick bathroom break, Mrs. Leita was sitting in the reception area wiping tears from her eyes. I sat next to her and asked what was wrong. She opened her mouth but hesitated to speak. When I assured her, it was okay to talk, she said in a soft voice, *"Pastor Dev is cheating on me, and I don't know what to do. I found a 10-hour recording on one of our old iPhones that we let Ashley play with. Ashley accidentally left the phone on. He spent the whole day on the phone with various women while I'm here slaving away."* She looked at me with fear in her eyes and begged me not to say anything to the ministry team. She said that she didn't know what he would do if he found out that she told me. I could tell Mrs. Leita was afraid.

I was confused, angry, and nervous at the same time, confused because the Pastor Dev I knew couldn't possibly do such a thing. Anger kicked in because this is the same man who beat us down about living righteously and not sinning, yet he was cheating on his wife. Then, I got nervous because I didn't want to say anything I shouldn't. Pastor Dev drilled into us that we dare not talk negatively about a man of God. All I could tell Mrs. Leita was everything was going to be alright. She begged me again not to say anything to the ministry team or her husband. She was convinced that everyone in the ministry would stand by him. The more the Pastor's wife cried, the madder I got. What was I supposed to do with this information?

The anger I felt wouldn't go away. I was in a crazy state of mind thinking about everything I was trying not to do: struggling to remain celibate, fighting to stay away from bad relationships, and sacrificing time with family and friends to do what Pastor Dev told me was right, but he was doing everything he told us not to do. Still, the fear that I would be cursed and get sick for leaving the church prevented me from doing anything. Though I had no proof, I believed Mrs. Leita. The hurt and tears weren't fake; betrayal and fear were written all over her face.

I didn't speak a word to anyone about what Mrs. Leita told me and continued to check on her to make sure she was okay. She started to share other things going on in the church and at home. Mrs. Leita confided in me that the way Pastor Dev treated us was nothing compared to his disrespect towards her. The name calling was nothing new to her. Initially, hearing this information was uncomfortable, once the dots started to connect, I no longer felt conflicted listening to Mrs. Leita and worrying about Pastor Dev finding out.

In fact, listening to Mrs. Leita sparked a light. I wasn't 100% sure, but I felt Pastor Dev lied to us about many things. It all made sense; how could I expect Pastor Dev to treat us with respect when the woman he professed to love was being treated miserably at home? He was supposed to be our leader, but to him, we were weak, broken people he controlled. Mrs. Leita shared with me that Pastor Dev always referenced Jenna and me during their arguments; he would ask her if she wanted to end up divorced, alone, and living miserable lives like us.

Every week, I learned about something Pastor Dev did or was doing from Mrs. Leita. He openly told us the importance of tithing every Sunday, yet he was taking tithe money from the very individuals he told us didn't tithe. I saw random envelope exchanges from members on the ministry team directly to Pastor

Dev. I wondered why it was okay for us to place our tithe in the offering receptacle during service, but they handed envelopes to him instead. Since I was new to the church, I dismissed the thought. However, Mrs. Leita explained that she would find those same envelopes, empty, with members' names on them.

To make matters worse, I was struggling to pay my bills. I was stuck in a cycle of payday loans every week. I thought I was wrong for thinking the ministry team investment was too much, but we did not see much going out. For example, every week we had fundraisers, but we didn't receive any of the profit to replenish the items we purchased. I didn't expect to get money back, but I thought the fundraisers would eventually fund itself. For events, the ministry leadership bought the food, gifts, and decorations. I'm not accusing the church of stealing, but we were abused spiritually and financially. Only seven of us, other than the Pastor and his wife, consistently provided funds to support the weekly fundraisers and church events. The ministry team purchased the ingredients, and each person brought a dish. We also paid for the food we ate. If we didn't have money that week we could pay later. Of course, my tab stacked up. On so many instances, I went without to help the church. I even lied to siblings for help to pay my bills.

One night, the ministry team was decorating at the church for our fall festival. I was on a ladder in the sound area decorating the wall, when suddenly, I lost my balance and fell off the ladder. Fortunately, the mixer broke my fall. I gashed the side of my leg from the fall, but I didn't break anything. Ariel called Pastor Dev and told him what happened. She explained I was fine, and the mixer just had a small dent. He told us to be careful and wrap up for the night.

The following evening, we had dance rehearsal for our upcoming fall festival. When Pastor Dev arrived, he looked at the mixer and said there wasn't just a dent in the mixer. The buttons shifted on the board. He was concerned the mixer wouldn't work properly the day of the event. Then, he accused me of being careless for not moving the mixer out of the way. He asked, *"If you had something of value wouldn't you move it out of the way?"* I said, yes. He continued talking. *"Well, you didn't value the ministry equipment enough to move it out of the way."* I immediately looked up the mixer online; Amazon had it for $200. I told Pastor Dev that I would pay for it. But, he said buying used equipment was not trustworthy and told me to replace the mixer; the cost was $3,000. Pastor Dev said since four of us were present that night, we had to split the cost. We had 24 hours to come up with $750 apiece. I had no idea how I was going to get that money in a short period of time. I ended up using my rent money, which was exactly $750. One leader was unable to come up with her amount, so Pastor Dev said I had to cover her portion. She agreed to pay me back later. I got a $550 payday loan and asked my older sister to borrow $200. Ariel shared that she lied to her parents and told them she couldn't pay her rent, so they gave her $750. I'm not sure what Jenna did, but we all had our portion within the 24-hour period. The day of the event, the same mixer that was supposedly broken was used to run the sound system, but new lights and a fog machine were purchased.

Shortly after the mixer incident, everything was chaotic. Ariel was managing more than 20 kids for hours at a time. Pastor

Dev asked members of the church to volunteer a few hours a day to help Ariel with the kids while I worked. Mrs. Leita started showing up later each day. When she showed up, the workday was almost over. Some days, Ms. Leita tried to work; other days, she just needed someone to talk to. I did my best, but directing an academy was new to me. Mrs. Leita usually handled the money and double checked my record keeping. I was so tired and overwhelmed that it started to affect my remote job and the academy. I had several warnings from my supervisor that I wasn't doing well. Pastor Dev thought I was distracted again, but my drive to do anything was gone.

I was depressed and didn't know it. Church records were not being completed consistently anymore. I wasn't answering my work calls like I was supposed to. I got tired of being a bill collector for parents who didn't pay their academy bill. I was working on grant reimbursements at the end of the month instead of daily record keeping. I wanted to leave but was scared.

For three years, I gave my all to the ministry. I wanted to quit, but I didn't want my life to be cursed as Pastor Dev put it. All kinds of thoughts came to my head: *How would I start over? Would I be in the same state, lacking purpose?* I didn't know how I would survive outside the four walls of The Worship Center on my own. I ran most of my decisions by Pastor Dev first. I consulted him on everything from looking for a new job to getting a new car to whom I would date in the future. Pastor Dev became my crutch. We were led to believe that he heard from God for us, so I couldn't think for myself anymore.

11. WHO'S YOUR GOD?

"How you doing? It's been a long time?" The text message from Chris popped up on my phone. The last time I talked to him was nearly four years ago. Considering everything going on, I thought it would be a great change to connect with an old friend. I knew hanging out with a guy would be a huge no for any of us in The Worship Center leadership team, but I no longer cared. Since Pastor Dev was a liar and a cheater, I thought, *who cares what he thinks*. It was Thanksgiving weekend, and Pastor Dev wanted us to come to his house for the holidays. We were taught to believe it's always an honor to be in the presence of a man of God, so we should never turn down opportunities to be around Pastor Dev. But, I stood my ground that day and told him I had a lot I needed to get done. Truth was I knew Chris was coming into town that night and wanted to hang out. I thought nothing would happen because I'd been celibate for three years, but I underestimated my weakness and ended up sleeping with him. I literally felt like my chest was on fire. The overwhelming feeling of guilt and pain wouldn't go away. I could not believe what I had done; I had broken my vow of celibacy.

I cried out to God for forgiveness. In that moment I heard an audible voice say, *Who's your God?* God was not only exposing

Pastor Dev, but He also was showing me my heart. I began to see that I was only able to remain celibate because I had no idle time to fall into sin; the commitment I had made did not keep me out of trouble. I kept thinking how could I let God down like that, but the truth was my celibacy wasn't because of my reverential fear of God; it was the result of my fear of a man. A man I called my Pastor. I realized that I feared Pastor Dev more than I feared God.

The next day, I was on pins and needles at Pastor Dev's house, thinking he would find out what I'd done. Though I heard what God said to me, I was still gripped by fear. Pastor Dev had a strong hold on me mentally. I went to church in shambles the following day, full of guilt and shame. I tried to put on my poker face, but I failed miserably. It wasn't long before Pastor Dev realized something was wrong. When he took the stage, I didn't hear a word he preached that morning. At the end of service, Pastor Dev said, *I sense the ministry team needs prayer*." I think he didn't want to call me out, so he asked the leaders to come to the altar for prayer. As he went down the line, Pastor Dev laid hands on everyone, and they all started falling out. When he prayed for me, he placed his hand on my head three times. While everyone around me fell to the ground, I stood at the altar and cried hysterically due to the enormous guilt I felt. After the service, I stayed away from greeting and talking to members. Once everyone left the church, the ministry team sat down to have lunch. I noticed Pastor Dev acknowledging everyone but me at the table. I knew I was in trouble.

I left church before the evening service to purchase items needed for the academy. When I returned, Pastor Dev said his son AJ was screaming in his sleep. When Jenna asked what happened, Pastor Dev said the spirits he cast out of me during the service were lingering in the building and tormented his son because children are susceptible to demons. I looked up at him and said nothing. The explanation sounded stupid and scary at the same time. I didn't know if Pastor Dev was trying to manipulate me into telling him what was wrong or if he was telling the truth. Either way, I wasn't ready to tell him anything. When Jenna asked what type of spirits they were as if she was afraid, Pastor Dev said more than nine spirits were cast out of me, but he didn't name them. I knew that I would get the silent treatment until I told him what I had done.

Once the evening service was over, I asked Mrs. Leita and Pastor Dev if I could speak to them privately. I told them everything that happened between Chris and me. Pastor Dev asked what I was thinking. He said he didn't want to embarrass me in front of everyone, but the spirit of lust was heavy on me. Mrs. Leita asked if I wasn't afraid of getting some type of disease. I told her I didn't expect anything to happen. Pastor Dev then said, *"That's why you've gained weight around your hips and caring about the way you look"*. I was confused and in utter disbelief because I was with Chris two days prior to telling them what happened. Pastor Dev made me feel worse than I did prior to walking into their office. Now, changing my hairstyle and the way I looked was the reason I fell into sin.

Everything got flipped around, and I couldn't even remember the original issue. Pastor Dev sighed and asked if I wanted to continue the same cycle. I shook my head no because I couldn't stop crying long enough to give a verbal response. He asked if

I really liked the guy and what his intentions were. I answered yes, but I knew Chris and I couldn't have more than that night we shared. When I asked Chris, what was going to come of the situation, he told me a long-distance relationship doesn't last. He asked if I was willing to travel to see him. I knew being at The Worship Center wouldn't allow me to travel, so I sadly said no.

However, I didn't tell Pastor Dev and Mrs. Leita the conversation I had with Chris. Pastor Dev instructed me to invite Chris to the church and asked me his profession. When I shared that Chris was a teacher, Pastor Dev asked, *"Is that all you want for yourself?"* as if teaching wasn't a worthy profession. Before I could respond, Mrs. Leita interjected and said, *"In the U.S., that's a good profession to have."* I knew the whole counseling session was wrong. I was scared to tell them that I wasn't inviting Chris to the church, so I told them that I reached out to him, but he was not interested in visiting the church or pursuing a relationship with me. Pastor Dev hugged me and said it would be okay. He claimed the guy didn't want anything but sex, so I should not beat myself up about it.

12. DANGER

I arrived at Pastor Dev's house a little after midnight. I pulled up to flashing red and blue lights. Freaked out, I ran up the driveway to Mrs. Leita standing at the entrance of her garage with two officers going back and forth on their walkie talkies. When I asked what was wrong, she said, *"Please take care of my babies I have to go. I've been trying to reach Pastor Dev for several hours."* She scrolled through her phone to show me over 50 outbound calls. Mrs. Leita said she felt like she was about to lose her mind. I reassured her everything was okay and called Pastor Dev as well, but he didn't answer.

The officers wanted to know who I was. When I explained I was a member of the church and her husband was the pastor, they asked if I would be able to stay with the kids or they would have to call protective services. I assured them there was no need because I could help her and the children. Mrs. Leita turned around and said she didn't want to harm her kids, but she felt like she wanted to die and take the kids with her. I asked the officers where they were taking her. They gave me the name, so I could give the information to Pastor Dev. Before Mrs. Leita left, she asked that I please take care of the kids. The officers informed me the dog was blocking the door and wanted to know if I would have difficulty entering the home. I told them I would be fine.

I could hear AJ screaming "Saaana" from the garage door. I was trying to get inside, but I was afraid of the dog, so I stayed where I was. I kept calling Pastor Dev…no answer. I called his assistant Tim, who showed up 30 minutes later. The dog let him in, so I was able to make sure the kids were fine. Ashley was sitting on the couch while AJ was in his playpen crying. An hour and half later, Pastor Dev called. I explained that Mrs. Leita had called the police and was being Baker Acted. When Pastor Dev finally arrived, I told him where his wife was. I called the facility for him and was able to reach Mrs. Leita, but she had to wait 24 hours to be released. Pastor Dev instructed me that I shouldn't share what happened to the ministry leadership because they would lose respect for her. When I asked if he needed me to stay with the kids, Pastor Dev told me he would be fine. The next day Mrs. Leita was released, and things returned to functional chaos. Mrs. Leita never talked about that night again.

Pastor Dev was still sending indirect messages through his sermons. This time, his wife was the target as well as me. He started his message that day by saying *"There is no such thing as trust; focus on doing what God wants you to do."* I looked over at Mrs. Leita; all I saw was a blank stare as she listened to Pastor Dev preach. I rolled my eyes and sucked my teeth while sitting in the front row. Of course, no one saw me. I couldn't believe he was indirectly speaking to me while trying to manipulate his wife. At this point Mrs. Leita told me he didn't want to address the 10-hour recording of him talking to various women. Pastor

Dev told the congregation all a person needed was love, so trust wasn't a factor.

A few days prior to this message on love, I commented that I could not be with someone I did not trust. He made sure to address my comment from the pulpit. If I had any doubt that Pastor Dev was cheating on his wife, he removed it all with his message. I looked around and wondered if anyone really believed what he was saying.

I was so comfortable in the organized chaos that I never questioned why the heck I still sat there listening to what I knew was wrong. What's so sad is Pastor Dev used the example of a husband cheating on his wife as an explanation of what loving a person looked like and how trust didn't matter. He said, "*A woman should do her wifely duties and even if a husband messed up, he would come to her and tell her the truth about what he had been doing and that there was no need to play detective or nag him. God would take care of it, just continue with your regular duties.*" With his message, Pastor Dev confirmed everything Mrs. Leita told me about him. He was working his agenda while misleading the congregation. Instead of walking away from the situation, I couldn't muster the courage to leave.

Mrs. Leita continued to confide in me as her situation progressively worsened. I worried about being out of order because Pastor Dev was my spiritual leader, but as a woman, I couldn't help but be compassionate. I suggested they both seek counseling. When Mrs. Leita scheduled an appointment, Pastor Dev wasn't willing to go because he didn't think anything was wrong with him. I encouraged Mrs. Leita to attend the counseling session for herself. It was exhausting telling her everything was going to be fine. With every passing day, her situation escalated. Sadly, Pastor Dev treated his wife like a doormat.

Our venting sessions became about our misery with no resolution in sight. One day, I told Mrs. Leita to stand up for herself and call Pastor Dev out on his mess. She responded that she was afraid of his anger and what he was capable of. I completely understood her fears. She was in a difficult position. Mrs. Leita had no support while everyone around her rallied for Pastor Dev. I was preaching to myself. I told Mrs. Leita to confront her situation but I wasn't addressing how Pastor Dev treated me. I was passed the phase of guilt that I may be judging him. I just didn't have the boldness that I was telling Mrs. Leita to have. I knew deep down that a man whose house was in shambles couldn't effectively lead me or anyone else. I had to believe that God would fix everything even though I couldn't see it. I did my best to encourage Mrs. Leita to do what I couldn't, be bold. She expressed being afraid, but I didn't anticipate any danger.

Mrs. Leita, Jenna, and I locked up the church around 9:00pm that evening. Shortly after I got home, I called Jenna. I had to tell someone how I felt. Although we weren't as close as we wanted to be, we both could see a lot about Pastor Dev that others couldn't. I confided in Jenna that I wanted to leave The Worship Center. She told me it wasn't a good idea. Jenna tried to convince me that everything would be okay. I asked her to hold on because Mrs. Leita was calling me.

I clicked accept on the facetime call to see my Pastor's wife's bloody face crying. Immediately, she said, *"He hit me; I wanted you to know just in case he tries to kill me. He's coming back; I have to go!"* I clicked over to Jenna and told her that I had to call the police because Mrs. Leita had a bloody face. Though Jenna told me not to do it, I hung up the phone and called the police anyway. She didn't see what I just witnessed. Blood was all over Mrs. Leita's face. There was no way I could live with myself knowing that she reached out to me for help, and I didn't do anything. I couldn't remember their address when the dispatcher came on the line, so I gave the dispatcher Mrs. Leita's phone number and the street they lived on.

When I called Jenna back, she told me I was wrong for calling the police. Less than five minutes later, Pastor Dev called me. I didn't answer the phone, but he called four more times. I still didn't answer. I told Jenna I didn't know what to do. I wanted to make sure I was calm before I called him back. Fifteen minutes later, I called Pastor Dev. *"Where the f**k were you?"* he shouted. *"I was in the shower,* I said. *"Did you call the f**king police on me?"* He didn't give me an opportunity to respond. He continued shouting *"The officers told Mrs. Leita that her friend Sandra called and said she needed help."* Before I could answer I heard Mrs. Leita in the background yelling, *"The officers didn't say your name."*.

So many questions raced through my head. I thought about the gun he owned. *What if he tried to kill me? What if he got arrested? What if he got deported?* I was freaking out. Pastor Dev hung up the phone without saying a word. I thought I should leave my apartment, but I had no idea who I could call. My car had a flat tire, so I was stuck. It was around 11:00pm. I couldn't call my family because they would freak out. Thirty minutes later, Pastor Dev called back and said, "*I thought you were the one who called the police because you were the last person in [Leitas] call log.*" I later found out that Mrs. Leita covered for me and told him that she accidentally dialed my phone number when he tried to take her phone. I kept my composure and denied calling the cops.

Pastor Dev seemed to flip a switch. He acted as if nothing happened and told me he was on his way to pick me up to help Mrs. Leita with the kids because she wasn't feeling well. I thought if I said I couldn't go; he would suspect I knew what happened. So, I said okay then called Jenna and told her that Pastor Dev was picking me up to help Mrs. Leita. I wanted someone other than Mrs. Leita to know what was going on in case something happened to me.

When Pastor Dev pulled up to my apartment, I had no idea what to expect. I quickly went to his car and sat on the passenger's side quietly. He shared some lame story that he and Mrs. Leita got into an argument and she fell over gym equipment in the garage. He claimed that he tried to leave the situation, but a neighbor called the police. Their argument outside turned out to be my saving grace. Mrs. Leita later told me the neighbor was trying to figure out if she was okay, but she ran into the house before she was seen.

As Pastor Dev tried to explain what happened, Ariel called. He told her to come and pick me up because he was late for his supplement appointment. Pastor Dev recently started body building as a hobby and told us the process required a weekly injection to help him build muscle. Apparently, his supplier had to administer the injection in Miami. The story was strange because it was well after midnight. I thought to myself, *He just beat his wife and now he was going to an appointment after midnight.* I didn't believe him. When he drove off, I had the thought to empty my office and never speak to them again, but how could I leave Mrs. Leita hanging like that. I dismissed the idea because I didn't know who to call for help. When Ariel picked me up, I didn't say anything to her. She could not be trusted. I knew she wouldn't think twice about telling Pastor Dev what I knew. She didn't even question why she had to pick me up well after midnight.

I walked into the house and saw Mrs. Leita sitting at the kitchen table with a bloody towel on her nose. I did not want Tim and Ariel to think I knew more than they did, so I texted Mrs. Leita and asked how she was feeling. I got angry all over again as I watched Tim, who lived with them, walk around the house as if Mrs. Leita were invisible. Ariel simply sat on the couch and didn't ask if she was okay. I had insight on what was going on, but any human being with a beating heart could tell something was wrong.

Mrs. Leita texted me that her nose might be broken. I told her she should go to the hospital and get checked out. She agreed, so around 2:00am, she called Pastor Dev to tell him that I was taking her to the emergency room. He didn't call back. Instead, he texted Mrs. Leita that all she needed was aspirin; the hospital was not needed. I advised her to go and make sure that she was okay. Pastor Dev was against it but we went to the emergency room anyway. He didn't come to the hospital nor call while we were there.

When the doctor entered the room, Mrs. Leita explained that she hurt her nose from a fall. X-ray results showed she had multiple fractures. The doctor asked, "Are you sure those fractures are from a fall?" Mrs. Leita said, "Yes." I gave her a look of *This is your time to say something*. But, she ignored me and continued to assure the doctor that it was an accident. A few minutes later, a social worker walked into the room. I scrolled through my phone to avoid eye contact with the social worker. Mrs. Leita said she was fine and declined further assistance.

We spent six hours in the emergency room in silence. I broke the silence by telling Mrs. Leita that I wanted to leave The Worship Center because I couldn't handle what I knew. I noticed Mrs. Leita's demeanor change as she adjusted her position on the hospital bed. She didn't say a word. Somehow, I knew I should have kept that thought to myself. I tried to get some sort of reaction out of her, so I told her that I wasn't attending service that upcoming Sunday. In three years, I'd never missed a service. I knew that would get Pastor Dev's attention. Mrs. Leita looked at me and said, *"That's the same thing he would do."* I cringed, but I knew she was right. I was using a manipulative tactic to get Pastor Dev's attention instead of walking away from the situation.

Finally, Mrs. Leita spoke: *"When you are close to a man and woman of God, you will begin to see things about them that might not seem right to you, but you shouldn't run away."* With those words, I realized she was against me leaving. Mrs. Leita explained that when they were in India, they got close to one of Pastor Dev's uncles. They didn't agree with some of his actions. According to Mrs. Leita, the uncle and his family were different behind closed doors. She wanted to leave the church, but they decided to talk to the uncle and after their discussion, she and Pastor Dev realized that they were the problem. She explained they were focused on a person instead of God. I felt badly, but at the same time, I knew it was Mrs. Leita's way of trying to get me to stay. Something changed after that day. I no longer felt comfortable being as open with Mrs. Leita. I thought it was strange that she urged me to stay but wanted out of her marriage. Why would I want to be around someone she could no longer bare living with it?

When we walked out of the hospital, the academy was already open, so I had to start work immediately. I didn't even have time to drop Mrs. Leita home. We went directly to the church because it was nearly 8:00am. Pastor Dev didn't arrive at the church until 2:00pm with their kids. He sent Ariel, who had no idea what was going on, home. He instructed her to meet us at the academy within a few hours. Mrs. Leita set up a pallet next to her office desk and slept for most of the day. When I checked on her, I noticed the increased swelling around her eyes and how disoriented she looked. Pastor Dev told the ministry team not to bother her because she wasn't feeling well.

Meanwhile, I sat in my office struggling to work. I couldn't stop thinking about what Pastor Dev did to his wife. I worked for a few hours then decided to check on Mrs. Leita again. She sat up for a few minutes and told me the pain was too much. She asked Ariel to keep Ashley and AJ out of the office because she didn't want them to see her face. I had so many questions. The events of that day did not line up, so I asked her what happened with the officers. Mrs. Leita explained that when they knocked on the door, Pastor Dev told her that she was going to break up their family and the kids would be taken away from them. The police said they received a call about a domestic dispute, out of fear, Mrs. Leita denied the allegations. Pastor Dev used the children to manipulate her. I explained that he would have gone to jail, and she could have filed a restraining order against him. Mrs. Leita said she just wanted to move on and take care of her kids. The look of defeat on her face was a sign that she needed to rest. I said I would check on her periodically and went back to work.

A few days later Mrs. Leita convinced me to meet with Pastor Dev and share my concerns. Of course, my concerns had nothing to do with him beating her. Six months prior, Pastor Dev randomly instructed the ministry team to text him when Mrs. Leita arrived and left the church because she was emotional, and he wanted to make sure that she was safe. I thought it was weird, but we did what he said. In Mrs. Leita's office, Pastor Dev sat across from us. He reclined the chair and asked what I needed to discuss. I shared that I no longer felt comfortable texting him when his wife arrived and left the church because it was a violation of her privacy. Texting him her whereabouts had nothing to do with ministry.

Mrs. Leita disclosed to me that the ministry team had to text Pastor Dev when she came and went because she caught him in a lie. I remember the exact day. I intentionally did not text him that Mrs. Leita left, and Jenna didn't see her leave. Well, when Mrs. Leita arrived home, her husband wasn't there. She called him, and he said that he was in the house relaxing. Yet, he was nowhere to be found. It was the middle of the day; Pastor Dev didn't expect his wife to come home, and no one sent him a text. Later, he came to the church yelling at us about not texting him, but we had no clue why he was so upset. I lied and told him that I didn't see her leave. Now, it all made sense to me. Once I knew that was the reason we had to send text updates; I wanted to tell him I wasn't comfortable keeping tabs on his wife.

Pastor Dev responded to me with the words, *"That's fine if you don't want to be obedient to what the man of God is saying. Remember that obedience is better than sacrifice. Your lack of obedience should be taken up with God."* I started crying because I was confused and scared at the same time. I thought, *how was I being disobedient? What did a text message have to do with my obedience to God?* I couldn't remember what else I needed to say. Somehow, I managed to regroup and find my voice again. *"Why can't [Mrs. Leita] text you on her own,"* I said. He looked shocked that I asked. As his eyes turned red he defensively shouted, *"Don't approach me with your suspicious women bulls**t.* I leaned back in my seat and sat quietly. His tone let me know that he was done with that topic.

I couldn't decide what to do next. I felt that I was being suffocated. I sighed and continued with my concerns. *"Pastor Dev you don't have to call me a bitch or whore to correct me; simply telling me I'm wrong is enough,"* I said. I could tell he was frustrated as he responded, *"I will stop trying to help you; it's clear that you don't need my help. I'll just let you live your life how you please."* Yet again, the questions circulated in my mind. *Does this mean he wouldn't correct me when I'm wrong? Would I not get the proper training that I needed to be effective in ministry?* The tears started flowing again because I was confused and feeling all types of emotions. I really didn't understand where this conversation was headed. Nothing was being resolved. Pastor Dev looked at me and stated that he was simply preparing me. When I asked, *"Preparation for what?"* I sensed the agitation and anger as he said, *"What if your husband calls you a bitch; what are you going to do then?* I defensively responded, *"Why would my husband call me a bitch?"*

Then, Pastor Dev's whole demeanor changed. His eyes started to get red as he shared that the ministry team didn't understand his heart. He explained that he had to be tough on us to gain our respect. If he shared his heart with us, we would take advantage and be too casual with him. Tears began to roll down his face as he shared that he just wanted the best for me. He described how I went from not knowing the direction of my life to helping run an academy alongside his wife as a director. I was an emotional wreck, not because of his so-called moment of sensitivity, but because I was emotionally drained and confused regarding what was happening. One minute, he was angry with me. The next moment, he was emotional. He only started to cry when Mrs. Leita told him I wanted to leave the church. It suddenly hit Pastor Dev that he had to change the mean guy tactic. I walked out of the office more confused than ever.

13. GOD INTERVENES

On January 18, 2016, I wrote in my journal for the first time in three years... *"I've made a decision today that every day will be intentional. Everything will begin with God. I will make it a priority to talk and learn about God daily. I will fall deeply in love with the Man who has yet to let me down. I'm intentionally working hard for the kingdom. I'm intentionally living my life as the woman who will one day be a wife, a mother, and everything else that God has laid out for me. I will intentionally work on consistency, discipline, my character, and being that virtuous Proverbs 31 woman. I will write it all down and make [it] very clear. I'm remembering that where there is no vision the people perish. I talk a lot with no action and no fruit. Finances, Health, Fitness, Relationships, everything will be laid out and intentional. This is the beginning.*

I kneeled at the edge of my bed and told God I didn't know what I was feeling, but I needed Him more than ever. I just wanted to get close to Him. I was willing to do whatever it took. When I got up from my prayer, I laid in bed thinking how I could effectively manage my time to read my Bible and pray like I should. I was determined to do better. My plan was to look past everything going on and focus on my relationship with God.

Suddenly, my phone's ringer startled me. I was surprised to see my sister-friend Diana calling. We hadn't spoken in almost 6 months. When I answered the phone, Diana's first question was "*Sis, what's wrong?*" I couldn't bring myself to tell her everything happening at The Worship Center. She knew right away that something was wrong with me. I told her I felt that my relationship with God was not where it should be, but I knew she wasn't convinced. Diana told me that God laid it on her heart to share a video with me and that she would be praying for me. I told her to send the video. I was overwhelmed with my thoughts, so I didn't open the link to watch the video. I laid in bed for the rest of day thinking about my life and what was next.

The following day I could not focus on work. Pastor Dev and Mrs. Leita were in the lobby talking; I stopped working and decided to talk to them. I didn't quite know what I was going to say, but I knew I was miserable. I walked out of my office and leaned against my door. "*What wrong?*" asked Pastor Dev. "*I feel like I shouldn't be here anymore,*" I said. *I'm just not happy. God showed me that I look to you more than I look to Him for answers.*" Mrs. Leita seemed shocked by my words, but Pastor Dev responded, "*I knew that, but only God could show you that you had to put Him first.*" I ignored his response because I knew it was a lie. I continued sharing some of my feelings: "*I'm so desperate for answers from God that I've even gone to my closet early in the morning for prayer and tried to fast.*" As they both laughed, Pastor Dev gave me this drawn out explanation: "*You don't need to pray in your closet and fasting is not needed. Just keep working and everything will be okay. Christians must be careful with fasting because it's spiritual. You open yourself up to a spiritual realm of good and evil. You are at your weakest during a fast and the devil comes to tempt. Don't take fasting lightly. For your safety one to three days is all you can handle when the time is right.*" I found myself in another irritating conversation with no helpful outcome. I simply responded, *"I gotta get back to work."*

A few days later I was driving down the interstate headed to church when the conversation with Diana suddenly popped in my head. When I arrived at my office, I put my headphones on in case someone walked in without notice and watched the video. I didn't recognize the man speaking, but he discussed signs that a person may be in a cult or under a controlling Pastor. The first time I watched the video, the signs described my exact situation. The man in the video said a controlling Pastor would say if you left the church you would be cursed or sick. He also talked about isolation. When I finished the video, I could identify with a least 30 of the 40 signs mentioned. Yet, I was in denial; I thought, *there was no way that I, Sandra Pierre, was part of a cult.*

It was written all over my face that something was wrong. When Jenna walked into my office, I didn't even let her speak. Instead, I insisted that she watch the video. I gave her the link and told her to watch it right away. Jenna came back and said, *"Wow, this is our church!"* I tried to dismiss everything I had just heard by telling myself all the signs didn't apply, so maybe I shouldn't give the video much weight. It didn't work; there was no way I could forget what I just heard. I didn't know how to do it, but I knew it was time to leave. I called Diana and told her everything going on at The Worship Center. She said she was on her way to pick me up, but I told her it wasn't that simple because my name was tied to a few things. For three days, Diana called me to see if I was ready to walk away. She offered to help me find someone who could guide me out of the situation. I needed all the help I could get because I was utterly confused.

On a Wednesday afternoon, I went to Pastor Dev and Mrs. Leita to tell them I didn't think I should be at The Worship Center anymore. I never shared the video I watched. They asked me to sit down and talk to them. I knew the conversation wasn't going anywhere, and I would be manipulated into staying at the church. I stated that I did not have anything to discuss. As they repeatedly asked me what was wrong with me, I repeatedly said I didn't know. A part of me hoped they would tell me to leave. Pastor Dev reminded me that I had a history of running away from my problems instead of addressing them head on. I still didn't tell them anything. They closed the meeting stating that they would be there for me when I was ready to talk. Unfortunately, I thought I should tie up a few loose ends with the daycare before I walked away.

I did not have a car, so I had no choice but to stay for Bible study that evening. I knew the message was going to be directed towards me. Coincidently, that day Pastor Dev talked about what he called "the law of establishment" during Bible study. I paid close attention and took lots of notes. I didn't know exactly why I took the notes in that moment, but now I could share it as part of my story. The message that night went like this… *"Tonight, I would like to talk to you guys about the law of establishment. You guys have never heard me talk about this before. God is showing me that I need to teach you guys about the law of establishment. A lot of people in this ministry are struggling, but they won't speak up. If you leave the place that God has brought you to, your life will be cursed. He establishes you to bless you, but you will forfeit your blessing when you walk away from that place. You'll never walk in the blessings that God has for you. Women in America are pussies. They don't even know how to reach out for help when God has* *placed them in good counsel. Nothing you do will prosper. Even if you ever get married, your marriage will fail, your husband will divorce you. If you go to a different church, you will be sick because that's not where God placed you. What if the people of Israel decided that they didn't want to stay in Canaan? They would never have experienced the blessing that God already had planned for them. I am telling you exactly what God is saying. I've done my part; my conscious is free. I don't give a damn about your feelings. Feelings are bulls**t. That's your flesh, and it's not of God."*

The more Pastor Dev talked, the angrier he became. The members in the room who never heard him curse look shocked and confused. However, I didn't show any emotion. In fact, I sat through his message unbothered. I can't explain what happened to me that day, but I no longer felt Pastor Dev had a hold on me. I knew his message was meant to scare me into staying, but it had the opposite affect: it freed me. The madder Pastor Dev got, the more I realized his message had nothing to do with God. Whatever hold he had on me was finally broken. For the first time in years, I felt no fear as I listened to his message. In fact, the message made me stronger because I could see clearly.

Everyone else on the ministry team sat clueless about where the message came from. Since I took notes during the entire time, there was no indication that something was wrong. I knew Mrs. Leita was no longer on my side about confronting issues. The fact that I wanted to leave took the attention off their problems; they became a united front to keep me. For months, she did not participate in Bible studies; Mrs. Leita was only physically present. During the message that day, she raised her hand to comment on "the law of establishment." She confidently asserted that a person who left the place that God put them would miss out on the best God had for them. Her comment agitated me. I couldn't believe that Mrs. Leita really wanted me to stay under her husband's leadership with everything she knew about him. When the service ended, I cleaned up and talked to everyone, but said nothing to Pastor Dev. He left, and Mrs. Leita called me into her office and said Pastor Dev asked if I wanted to discuss anything. I maintained my composure and led on that I was fine. I just wanted to get home and figure out how in the world I was going to leave with no ties to them.

I felt that I had to pretend for my exit to go smoothly. So, I requested the rest of the week off from my remote job to get my workstation situated at home again. My plan was to complete the documents that had to be submitted for the academy, organize the weekly church attendance, file any documents as necessary, and so on. As I sat in my office, I was a nervous wreck, but according to my timetable, I could execute my plan as I laid it out.

I woke up Thursday, January 28, 2016, ready to execute my plan. I organized papers, cleaned the office, and continued answering calls for the academy. Diana called me and wanted to know if I had left the church. I assured her that I had a plan, but she advised me to leave as soon as possible. I replied that I wanted to do the right thing and finish what I started. Though she didn't' agree, Diana reassured me that she was there for me. Shortly after my talk with Diana, her Pastor, who was counseling me out of the situation, sent me a text. I shared what had transpired the night before during the Bible study. Diana's Pastor emphatically stated that I needed to forget my title and walk away. He explained that I would only continue to be broken down emotionally and spiritually, so I couldn't afford to be in that place anymore.

I decided to leave that day. I broke the news to Mrs. Leita first. She was in complete shock because she didn't say much. I explained that I would finish some paperwork before leaving. She went into her office, and I heard her on the phone. I knew she was talking to Pastor Dev. Less than an hour later he arrived at the church. Pastor Dev walked right past my office. Things started to get weird from that moment. Suddenly, they removed me from the ministry's group chat and rushed to respond to parents who came to pick up their children from the academy. They acted as if I was going to expose something. But, I simply wanted to leave; I wasn't trying to mess up what they already had going on.

The ministry team arrived at the church earlier than usual. They normally showed up well after 5pm but that day it was around 3 and 4 pm. I figured that Pastor Dev sent a mass text informing them that I was leaving the church. I texted Jenna that it was my last day, so she already knew. As I watched them walk by, no one said anything to me. Suddenly, I became afraid because everyone acted as if I didn't exist. I literally started trembling. I called one of my cousins who was scheduled to pick me up at the end of the day. Through tears, I told her that I was nervous and needed her to pick me up as soon as possible. As I waited in my office, I decided to thank Mrs. Leita and Pastor Dev for all the good things they did for me and times they helped me. The other leaders were in the academy area waiting to see what would happen, I guess. As I stood in Mrs. Leita's office, Pastor Dev replied that I was free to live my life as I pleased, and he would pray to release me before I left. I said okay and went to sit in my office while waiting for my cousin. I heard Pastor Dev consoling his wife, telling her that she didn't need to cry, and everything would be okay. Mrs. Leita responded, "*How could she do this to us; I treated her like a sister.*" I was stunned and couldn't understand what I did wrong.

An hour later my cousin finally pulled up, I told her not to come inside. I left everything in my office except my job's equipment. Before leaving, I asked Pastor Dev if I could I say goodbye to the rest of the ministry team. He waved his hand and said, "That's fine." Both Mrs. Leita and Pastor Dev were on my trail as I walked into the academy classroom. I hugged Jenna as she asked if I was really leaving. I replied that I had to go. When I tried to hug Ariel, she folded her arms and told me that she couldn't believe what I was doing. I shrugged my shoulders and walked away. Pastor Dev and Mrs. Leita stood by the exit door, and I handed them the keys to the building. He swung the keychain attached to the keys and told me that he wanted nothing that had to do with me. I smirked and told him the key chain belonged to them; his response and demeanor made my exit easy. I walked away with no intention of ever looking back. That night, Ariel called me crying to tell me that I was making a mistake. I replied that I knew she didn't understand why I left, but I couldn't say anything else. I wished her the best and hung up the phone.

The next day, I emailed the county, informing them that I was no longer affiliated with The Worship Center and to remove my name as the academy's director. I was concerned because Pastor Dev and his wife had all my information, including my social security number. However, there was nothing I could do but monitor my credit report. I tried to contact Jenna, but she wouldn't respond to me. I had a feeling that the Pastors turned her against me. I went to Jenna's job to ask why she wasn't answering my phone calls. She replied by asking me why did I talk about her? I assured her that I never did. I explained that the only person I shared things with was Mrs. Leita. If anything, that we both agreed something wasn't right with Pastor Dev. When I said that, it clicked that Mrs. Leita took our conversations out of context and flipped it to her advantage to make Jenna feel as if I was against her. I told Jenna it was a lie, and Pastor Dev did not have her best interest at heart. I described how he talked about her all the time and was out to get her too.

Later that evening, I had a missed call from Pastor Dev. He left a voicemail saying, *"Hello Sister Sandra. This is Pastor Dev, The Worship Center. I'm calling you. I have [Jenna,] [Ariel], [Leita], and all the church people with me. I'm on a speaker phone. I was told that you're talking behind me personally, trying to spoil my name and the church's name, and I have everyone here. If you really want to do something like that, I'd greatly appreciated it if you'd come face to face and talk to us. Please do not be a spoiler of God's house. I'm telling you if you have anything please come face to face and talk to all of us. We are here, and you know where we are. Please come and talk to us. Don't work behind and poison people's heart. Do not do that. Alright. We thought you left and that you were going to mind your business, but I see you going around talking to church believers and spoiling them. I have Jenna here complaining about you, saying that you told things bad about me to her. So, if you want anything please come here and talk. And please do not repeat it because this is very bad what you are doing. Please take care. Bye."* I called right back and said I was on the way, but when

I hung up the phone, I knew the idea was stupid because no one would believe me. Pastor Dev only put them on speaker phone to make it seem that I was wrong. I thought that Jenna, if no one else, would believe me because she knew everything I knew. They convinced her I was the problem and she didn't leave. I did not go to the church that night as Pastor Dev requested. January 29, 2016 was the last time I spoke to Pastor Dev or Mrs. Leita.

Rumors circulated about me. When a member of the church saw me out in public, they asked me if what Pastor Dev said about me was true. He accused me of stealing money from the church and wanted to break his family apart. Mrs. Leita told the church that I forced her into a mental institute to take her husband. Though I knew better, it didn't hurt any less. Whenever someone left the church, every action or word spoken was up for interpretation to justify why the person who left was not a good fit at the church. Pastor Dev led the members to believe that I was trying to close the academy and taint the church. To shut down any question's members may have had, I was accused of stealing more than $20,000 of the church's money.

PART II
RESTORATION

1. FORGIVENESS AND HEALING

I couldn't shake the pain and guilt that consumed me. It was as if scales instantly fell from my eyes the day I walked away from The Worship Center. I could see clearly that I hurt people. Although I was in pain, knowing how I hurt those close to me was even worse. I immediately wanted to make things right with all those I shut out of my life, my family, my friends, and my co-workers. I knew I was wrong and let the influence of someone I called Pastor control my entire life. My mind became my worst enemy because memories flooded me daily. I couldn't focus on how to process what I went through. The realization of being in a cult made me feel like hiding in a dark place. I was ashamed that I made this man I called Pastor my God. I asked God to forgive me, but I didn't know how to forgive myself.

I was embarrassed at the thought of anyone knowing I was part of a cult and willingly let someone treat me with such disrespect. I kept asking, *how was I going to face my friends and family*? I didn't know what to expect. The hardest part of apologizing to those I wronged was not knowing their reaction or the outcome. It probably wasn't the best idea to contact my friends and family without fully processing all I felt and went through over the past three years, but I took a chance and started reaching out to those I intentionally shut out.

 The first person I had to speak to was Mia. This is the friend who I ended our relationship via text at the beginning of my involvement with the cult. I didn't know if her number was still the same, so I contacted her brother. I was afraid of calling her directly in fear that she would go off on me or refuse to talk. So, I asked her brother to find out if she was willing to speak to me. When I received the okay, I called her and nervously asked for us to meet. She replied that she would let me know when she was available. I thought that was only fair. A week went by, but I didn't hear anything. When I called her again, I told her it was important that I meet her as soon as possible. Her response was still nonchalant, so I thought she wouldn't come. I begged her to just give me a few minutes of her time.

 When Mia heard me crying, she agreed to meet with me that night. I didn't know what to expect after three years. I sat at Starbucks on pins and needles. As soon as she walked in, I saw my God Babies and couldn't fight back my tears. I hugged them and marveled at how much they had grown. Mia looked at me and asked why I was crying. She was never that emotional friend, so I looked at her and said, "Really?" We both laughed and hugged each other. She sat the girls at another table, so we could talk privately. I apologized about shutting her out and started sharing some things I felt. Mia was receptive and said she knew all along that Pastor Dev was a major reason behind me shutting her out. We talked until Starbucks closed for the night. The relationship didn't get better overnight, but with time, we developed an even closer bond.

I couldn't believe the support I received from friends and family. The fear that no one would forgive me tried to prevent me from reaching out to those I hurt. I also had to be fine with the reality that everyone might not be willing to forgive me. I even reached out to Lori and apologized. Despite Pastor Dev's influence I owned up to my wrong. She was receptive and forgave me as well.

When I walked away from the cult, I deleted all apps and pictures associated with The Worship Center. A few months later, I had to use one of the deleted apps. When I opened the app, I saw an old notification of a message that was nearly two years old. The message was from Wanda, my friend who lived with me for a few months that I thought would join the Worship Center. I couldn't believe that I completely forgot what happened between us.

> *Wanda (July 24, 2014): "SOOO idk if you are gonna get this bc you have like three GroupMe contacts but seriously I am thankful for you. Even though our living situation didn't work out I have no hard feelings against you. Can't say a bad thing about you bc you have been a blessing to me. I apologize for all uncomfortable situations I put you in. You being uncomfortable in your own house was not my intention. I am sorry and pray that all is well with you."*

I didn't find that message by accident. I knew I had to apologize and make things right. So, I contacted Wanda that day. I didn't know what I was going to say, but I called anyway. The phone number I had didn't work, so I reached out to her through the app.

Me (Jan. 31, 2016): Hi Wanda, do u still use this GroupMe?

Wanda (Feb. 4, 2016): Yes

Me (May 2, 2016): Hi Wanda, if you are willing, I would like to meet and talk with you. Didn't know you responded. I tried to call you a few times.

Wanda (May 2, 2016): Sure, no problem. I'm off today if you are available before 8pm.

When Wanda agreed to meet me, I offered to take her to breakfast a few days later. I needed time to think. For some reason, I thought an apology was not enough, so I prayed and ask God for wisdom on what to say. When we met, Wanda was welcoming and receptive. I didn't make excuses. I apologized and let her know that she didn't owe me an apology because I was wrong for the way I treated her. Like everyone else I spoke to, Wanda said she knew I was being influenced by the Pastor. Sadly, Wanda and I didn't speak again after that day. I couldn't blame her.

I had to pray and ask God to not only heal me, but also to heal those I hurt. It took time to accept that I couldn't mend all relationships. I realized that peace didn't come from my friends and family forgiving me. My comfort had to come from knowing that, through repentance, God instantly forgave me.

This realization didn't come overnight. I found myself having to reject guilt and shameful thoughts daily. Some days, I just didn't want to pray, read my Bible, or talk to anyone. Social media, hanging out, and work could only distract me from dealing with issues for so long. Though no one knew, I saw myself slowly going into a dark place in my mind. I could no longer try to suppress my hurt and pain like I did in the past. Confronting all my issues meant I had to put in work. I had to WORK at developing my relationship with God. I had to WORK at consistently reading my Bible. I had to WORK at being transparent about my past. I had a choice to make. I had to decide whether I was going to accept that my life would always be a dysfunctional mess or seek God for better. I no longer wanted the illusion of happiness. I wanted the love, joy, and peace that I read and heard preached about from the Bible.

2. IT'S NOT ABOUT ME

I thought confronting my past meant dealing with those who hurt me and vice versa. The more I focused on my relationship with God, the more I kept thinking about Jenna and Ariel. I stopped fighting and really sought God about them. I recalled how they were both hurt when I left. Ariel wouldn't even hug me, and Jenna was in tears when I said my final goodbyes. The day I walked away I couldn't focus on anyone but me. Though I felt that I needed to connect with them again, I was afraid. So, for months, I struggled with fear: the fear of people, the fear of my past, and the fear of dealing with what made me uncomfortable. The thought of communicating with anyone who was part of The Worship Center scared me. I started reading every scripture on fear and continued to develop my relationship with God. I prayed that if it were God's will for me to connect with those two ladies again, He would open the door.

A few months passed, and I decided to unblock everyone from the cult while scrolling through Facebook one day. I no longer cared if they knew what was going on in my life because they could not control me, nor did I fear what they could do to me. As I unblocked everyone, I noticed Ariel's profile picture.

Something was different about her. She looked refreshed and happy. She also had a piercing that I didn't see while we were in the cult, so I started to click through her pictures to see if she was still at The Worship Center. As I scrolled, I knew she was no longer there because the recent pictures were with her family; she was having tons of fun.

I didn't hesitate to dial Ariel's number though I had no idea what I was going to say. The last time we spoke was almost five months ago. Surprisingly, Ariel answered the phone. We made small talk, but I could tell she was a little hesitant in what she said to me. Ariel kept her responses brief. I didn't mention anything about the cult and neither did she. The conversation was less than five minutes. When I got off the phone, I asked God, "What's next?" Weeks later, I remembered that before I left The Worship Center, Ariel gave me $45 to get her background check completed to continue working in the academy. I immediately texted her to tell her I still had the money she gave me. She asked if we could meet up. I offered to treat her to lunch so it wouldn't be a quick meet up.

At first, the meeting was awkward, and I did a lot of the talking. We both avoided the "The Worship Center talk." I knew I was going to have to do it, but I was afraid that Ariel would shut down. I also knew that I had nothing to lose. When I asked if she still attended the church, Ariel avoided my question. Instead, she shared that she was mad at me for leaving The Worship Center. She said, "*I had to pick up more of your work. I'm being real that's what I was worried about.*" I couldn't get upset that picking up duties was Ariel's only concern because we were treated like slaves. I probably would have felt the same exact way.

I asked again, "*Are you still at The Worship Center?*" Ariel looked down at her drink as if she didn't want to go there with me. Still staring at her drink, Ariel admitted that she didn't want anything bad to happen because she was talking about a man of God. I assured her that she was fine and did not have to be afraid anymore. I left a few months ago and nothing happened to me. I explained that Pastor Dev just used scare tactics to keep us at the church, but I could tell that she wasn't convinced. Ariel said she was confused and didn't know what was right and wrong but needed a break from the ministry. When I shared a few details of what went on while I was at The Worship Center, Ariel looked so uneasy that I changed the subject and tried to be positive. I told her we should keep in contact and hoped she would, but I wasn't certain. I left the restaurant that evening not knowing what to think.

A week later, I noticed one of the board members from The Worship Center while walking through a Sam's Club parking lot. I quickly turned down another isle, so they wouldn't see me. When I got to my car, I couldn't leave because I knew I had to stop running. God was dealing with my fear. So, I walked back towards the store. My heart felt like it was about to beat out of my chest. I had no idea what I was walking into. The woman stood right in front of the store talking to her daughter. I tapped the board member on her shoulder. When Mrs. Walter turned around, she placed her hand over her mouth in shock. When I leaned in to hug her, she responded with a tight squeeze. I couldn't believe how excited she was to see me. She looked at me with a concerned look and asked if I was okay.

SPIRITUALLY ABUSED AND BROKEN

Mrs. Walter and I sat down at the food court area as her daughter shopped. She said that she prayed for me all the time. I was open with her about why I left. She explained that she already knew something bad had to happen if I left the church. Mrs. Walter assured me that she didn't believe for a minute that I stole from the church. I was so relieved that someone believed me. When she asked had I heard from Ariel, I told her about our recent meeting. I could tell her heart broke for Ariel. I thought no one would ever believe that Pastor Dev was a completely different person behind closed doors. Mrs. Walter said she noticed the changes in his personality. Unfortunately, she was still attending the services every once and a while. Mrs. Walter's daughter was the alarm clock that alerted us an hour had passed. We agreed to stay in contact.

Part of my daily devotion was committing a Bible verse to memory. At the time I saw Mrs. Walter, the Bible verse that came to mind was "…fear not, for I am with you; be not dismayed, for I am your God; I will strengthen you, I will help you, I will uphold you with my righteous right hand" (Isaiah 41:10). I knew it was a reminder that God had my back, so I had no need to fear. The day after I saw Mrs. Walter, I received a call from Ariel, who shared that she and Mrs. Walter spoke for hours. *"I was afraid to tell you that I considered going back but after speaking to Mrs. Walter, I'm done"*, said Ariel Though she was on the fence, hearing what I went through and listening to Mrs. Walter explain the recent changes at The Worship Center gave her the strength to decide. Like me, Ariel was drawn in by the fact that Pastor Dev seemed to have a passion for God and people. She now saw for herself that we were deceived. One moment of obedience to move past my fear helped Ariel decide she wasn't returning to the cult. I thought, *how much longer would she have been deceived and hurt.* At this moment, I knew my story was no longer for me.

I believe that God wanted to solidify that He hears my prayers and was giving me the desire to help others stuck in abusive, controlling churches. Not long after seeing Ariel and Mrs. Walter, I was presented with another opportunity to reach someone else, at least that's what I thought. I walked into a dressing room to try on a few items when I heard a familiar voice. I listened a little bit longer and realized it was Jenna. I took a chance and walked out of the dressing room in search of where she was. I chuckled when I realized she was directly across from my dressing room.

Here was that open door I prayed about! I was amazed at how God works. As I knocked on the door, I said, "Jenna is that you?" When the dressing room door swung open, the look on Jenna's face was priceless as she exclaimed, *"San!!!!!!!! Is that really you? OMG, how are you girl? I can't believe it's you."* I was puzzled by her reaction and said, *"Jenna when I left, I thought you were mad at me. When Pastor Dev left the voicemail saying that you complained about me, I was confused but choose to leave it all alone."* She looked at me as if she didn't know what I was talking about. *"Girl, Pastor Dev still can't believe that you and [Ariel] are gone. You should see how the kids have grown. Pastor Dev has changed so much. We don't even stay at church late anymore, and things were completely different."* With no emotion I responded, *"Oh."* She proceeded to ask if I would visit the church. I said, *"No thank you."*

When Jenna asked me how I was doing, I shared that everything was great and told her that we should keep in touch. She replied, *"You know how it is when a person leaves the church."*

I thought, *does she realize what she just said*. The meeting was a heartbreaking reminder that people are misled and dying daily in these modern-day cults disguised as churches. I know that God didn't free me from a harmful situation to keep silent.

3. THE MESSENGER

In my quest to move forward quickly, I sought therapy and joined the church of the Pastor who counseled me out of the cult. The therapist was helpful, but I only had two sessions. I believed the sessions were focused on coaching instead of counseling and I didn't understand the difference at the time. Also, I didn't like that I had to remind the therapist what we discussed in our previous session; I felt like I was just an appointment on her calendar.

After a year attending the new church, I began to see and hear things that made me question whether I was in the right church. The integrity of the Pastor was discussed regularly by members, but my reaction is what scared me. I kept telling myself, He's a good person and has a good heart. I thought the very same thing even when I knew Pastor Dev was wrong. I was fearful of making another Pastor my God.

Though I felt it was time to leave, I did not do anything about it because I didn't want to be that person bouncing from church to church. I thought I did all the right things, but the reality was I jumped right into serving in the church instead of truly taking the time I needed to heal and trust not just my leaders but, most importantly, God. I had placed a band-aid over my wound instead of allowing it to breathe so that it could heal. I didn't want to end up in another cult.

I thought I had made a safe decision because the Pastor counselled me out of the cult and my friend Diana was there. Plus, I felt safe. I told God that I would trust Him where I was. Sounds silly now, but I really thought I could tell God what I was going to do in that moment. Pastor Dev's scare tactic that bad things would happen to me if I weren't covered by a leader continued to haunt me. I could not grasp that God had me covered. Though I repeatedly told myself that God would never leave or abandon me, I didn't really believe it in my heart.

The Pastor never made me feel uncomfortable and truly had a heart for people, but I ignored too much and didn't speak up about the things I saw. I kept telling myself that no one was perfect. Rumors continued to circulate about his integrity. Though I saw and knew too much, I wouldn't do anything because I tried to play it safe. I spoke up on certain things but left the hard stuff alone. I did not want to be hated. I wasn't a direct victim, but others were hurt and leaving the church left and right. Again, I prayed, but I didn't say anything.

God was gracious and revealed that I wasn't healed, nor did I mature spiritually from what I experienced in the cult. I had issues. I complained with others but sat in church as if everything were okay. Then, I masked my hypocrisy by telling myself that I shouldn't judge people. Things got so bad that I literally heard God say leave. For once, I did not delay leaving. A few days later after a Sunday service, I thanked the Pastor and his wife for their help and told them it was my last day. It was a déjà vu moment. Sadly, I didn't have the boldness to address why I had to leave.

I was already following another ministry prior to leaving the church. I told myself that I would not rush into anything new and decided to focus on hearing the weekly messages at this new church. Four months later, I found myself having an internal battle. I wanted to serve yet part of me felt that I should just chill more. Then came the guilt because I couldn't make up my mind. I went back and forth. Though my friends and family encouraged me that I would be okay, I was impatient throughout my healing process.

I simply wanted to get over everything and fully trust again, but there seemed to be no applicable steps to deal with all my issues. Question after question made me feel that I was losing my mind. Therapy was not an option because of the cost at the time; my friends and family could only do so much. My current Pastors counseled me, but I knew they were limited. Some days, I thought I was doing well, but days later, I found myself replaying some random situation with Pastor Dev and the church after that. I felt like I was on an endless emotional rollercoaster. I didn't know how to take hold of my feelings. I sank deeper into depression. I remember thinking, I must fight but was physically and mentally drained with life. A cloud of darkness seemed to hang over my head that I could not hide or run from.

It was a Sunday night. With the little energy I had, I tried to plan for the next day. Despite how I felt, I decided to be productive. I heard a knock on my bedroom door followed by the question, "Do you have some time to talk?" I said, "Yea, come on in." My roommate positioned herself on the ground across from me as I sat up on my bed to listen. She placed a pillow behind her back, sat Indian style, and shared that God had given her a prophetic message for me. I thought, here we go. My guard was up the minute I heard prophetic message. At this point I was tired of all the so-called messages she had from God prior to that day. When I asked what the message was about, she lifted a handful of papers and stated she had notes. Again, I asked what the message was about. I sensed Parisa's irritation as she blurted out that God had given her a mandate that I needed to vacate the premises within 30 days. I remained calm and said okay; I already knew this was coming.

I thought the conversation was over, but Parisa continued to ask when I would be ready to talk about the message God wanted her to give me. I took a deep breath and replied that I didn't know because I was in a vulnerable place. I explained that God's voice (His word) should be louder than anyone else's. What I said didn't click until later. I shared that she was more than welcome to leave the document for me to read when I was ready. I could tell Parisa was annoyed, so I said, "It's not that I'm not trying to receive what you have to say, but this is the state I'm in." I was putting up a front because I didn't want to hear what she had to say. Plus, I didn't want to make my remaining days uncomfortable. I preferred self-preservation over honesty at that time. Parisa got up and said she would be back because she needed to highlight and add a few notes. The nerve of this girl, I thought.

A few minutes later, I heard feet thumping up the stairs. I took a deep breath and answered after the second knock. I held the door ajar, took her notes and grudgingly responded "good night" as I closed the door behind me. I sat on my bed debating whether to read the document. I flipped through the typed notes in shock that it was 26 pages. I couldn't help myself; I wanted to know what Parisa could possibly say to me in 26 pages. I stared down at her notes titled "Prophetic Message. Stubbornness, Rebellion and Pride: Have you been delivered?"

When I met Parisa, I could have never imagined being in that weird place. We connected over similar interests. We were both foodies, so we enjoyed eating out and chatting about God and life. She was working on a book, and I had no idea where to start with the book I wanted to write, so I was excited because she gave me a lot of tips and insight on how to start writing. A year into knowing each other, I wanted to move out of my living situation, and Parisa allowed me to stay with her. The issues that seemed small when we lived apart magnified when we became roommates. Earlier, I encouraged her to be open about things that bothered her because she seemed to keep them inside; to me, it was obvious whenever she felt some type of way. At first, it was cool. She would share that certain things I said hurt her feelings. Then, it was the way I said certain things. I always apologized, and we moved on, but more incidents would pop up. As time passed, I felt that I was apologizing all the time and could never say the right thing. Then, I noticed during conversations if I didn't say something the way she thought it should be said, she corrected me in an indirect way. I had no problem being corrected or challenged, but I started to feel something wasn't right. I thought maybe she was trying to change me. So yes, I became defensive because I felt that being me was a problem.

As time went on, the issues amplified, and I constantly felt like a failure. It was draining to walk on pins and needles. I never knew when I would say something that hurt her. Finally, I let my frustration get the best of me. One morning, while helping Parisa prep for a wedding, she shared that I hurt her feelings the night before with my choice of words. Instead of saying "the problem is," I said "her problem is" therefore, I projected the issue. She said she knew God placed her in my life to not only help me with this book but to help me effectively communicate with her and my future husband. I let her finish, but I had enough. Parisa ended by saying that she had taken communication classes and wrote a book about it.

Once I finished her hair, I sat on Parisa's ottoman and asked what God was saying to her. Since I constantly heard what was wrong with me, I thought I would ask what God was saying to her about herself. I didn't feel she was being genuine. I shared with Parisa that I didn't need her to teach me anything, and I wasn't a little kid. I didn't realize that in that moment, I felt belittled and inferior to her. My emotions got the best of me. I told Parisa she had a wedding to get to and I was going to church. I walked away knowing I overreacted.

During my prayer time, God showed me two things: love is slow to anger and mercy triumphs over judgement. I immediately got up and apologized for my anger and the way I handled the situation. However, the situation escalated again, so I had to return and apologize again for my anger. This time, Parisa said she knew what she heard God say and basically, she was right, and I was wrong.

I found myself constantly asking God to forgive me and help me change if I was wrong. I kept my distance, and so did Parisa. I thought the situation cooled down. One day, while I was styling Parisa's hair, we made small talk. I shared a dream that I didn't understand. Parisa stated that she understood the dream and had asked God for an opportunity to speak to me; she felt it was the moment. She pulled out her journal and explained that she fasted three days for me. On each day, she prayed for a specific issue: pride, rebellion, and stubbornness. As I returned to doing her hair, Parisa said, "Don't shoot the messenger, I'm just telling you what God has shown me." I can't describe what I felt in that moment, but I just said okay.

I went up to my room asking, God, is this real? Like, I speak to you all the time and consistently ask you to show me any areas that I need to change. Are you really speaking to her? Am I wrong? Parisa's words weighed me down heavily. I prayed and said, "God, if I'm really those things, please help me." After I prayed, I knew I wasn't supposed to have a conversation with Parisa about what she shared. A part of me felt that she expected me to come to her and tell her that she was right. To avoid being wrong, I knew taking it to God in prayer was the right thing. I thought I let it go, but I still felt a heavy weight on me. My close friends told me that what Parisa was doing wasn't right, but I couldn't come to that conclusion. So, I walked away from that conversation feeling that I did something wrong; nothing could make me feel better. I felt tension every time I walked in the house.

Two months after the conversation regarding Parisa fasting about my issues, I tried to make small talk. We happened to meet in the kitchen at the same time eating food that her mother brought home. The conversation seemed okay to me at the time, but I was wrong. A few days later, I received a long text message explaining that I said something offensive and didn't realize that words have power. After I read the text message, I was in tears because I was fed up with the silent treatment and then a long text message telling me that I, yet again, did something wrong. In tears, I called Parisa to express that I didn't appreciate how she was treating me. In that moment, I felt that my pain was giving her power. I could hear it in her voice as she responded to my concerns.

Something Parisa said caught my attention, "God's not trying to punish you." I never felt that for one minute, so I spent time in prayer asking for help. Parisa, not God, was punishing me, and I felt it every time I walked in the house. Mid thought, I received a text message from Parisa stating, *"Hey so I'm texting this bc you're in school, but I just want to be clear that yes, I am keeping my distance bc I don't have to tolerate what hurts me. I obeyed God and pointed out what the issue is (speaking with grace, seasoned w salt, ect.) Stubbornness, Pride, and Rebellion (which manifest as anger) are blinding you from seeing the truth in what I'm saying. I don't mean to make you feel bad, but I must be obedient to God as far as what my response should be. Pls take it to God."*

Parisa started her 26 pages of notes by telling me that I was rebellious, prideful, and stubborn. The "prophetic message" was a gradual build of my life experience, weaknesses, and other information that I shared. Her notes centered around me being disobedient regarding being in beauty school, out of God's timing, and nine areas of development she felt I needed to focus on. Each area of development had several bullet points ranging from the way I dressed to the way I talked. It was as if Parisa kept surveillance on all our interactions without my knowledge, sat me down to review the footage, and told me what she saw needed to change. I felt violated, and there was no way to unread what I read. To top it off, her note ended by sharing that God instructed her to end our friendship because she was being elevated, and I didn't do the work to go with her. I felt that I was drowning in a pool of hurt, anger, insecurity, low self-esteem, inferiority, and doubt while rejection held my head under water.

I kept beating myself up after reading those pages, but if it weren't Parisa, it would have been someone else. I wasn't healed from being in a spiritually abusive cult, the church after that, and this situation with Parisa. My initial reaction wasn't pretty. I felt that I was being kicked, punched, and stabbed at the same time. I thought I was about to lose it. I even contemplated throwing hands, thinking, *how dare she come for me like that? Who does that?* I didn't know if I should cry or stay angry. I locked my bedroom door and prayed that Parisa wouldn't come back upstairs. I really didn't know how the situation was going to play out. Somehow, I managed to keep my composure and started packing my stuff. I knew that I couldn't spend another day, let alone 30 days in the same house with her. There was no way I could calmly address a 26-page document recording everything that Parisa thought was wrong with me.

I sent the document to my Pastors and told them that I was ready to fight. I knew I needed to get clarity on how to handle the situation because although I was leaving her home, we attended the same church. Within two days, I had moved out and tried to quickly move on, but the words on those pages would not leave my mind. I relived the cult experience all over; someone tearing me down in the name of God to prove a point. Though I could read between the lines and see that Parisa's issues were bigger than me, it didn't minimize the hurt I felt.

I had an internal battle. My initial thought was, *"She's wrong, this is all her...it's not God.* Then, I wondered was it really her or was there something wrong with me. I couldn't let go of the things that Parisa said about me. I found myself depressed and wanting to give up. I felt condemned and broken. Yet again, I subjected myself to being controlled with "God said" and scripture taken out of context. Parisa kept telling me that every chance she got, God would wake her up early to speak to her; she was a prophet of God, and people weren't honoring the prophet in her. In retrospect, those words were the red flags that something wasn't right, but I ignored them. I kept thinking; *she's doing me a favor by letting me stay in her home.*

The effects of the "prophetic message" left me mentally and emotionally drained. I couldn't go to church without thinking I was doing something wrong. Pride, rebellion, stubbornness, and any scripture used in Parisa's notes were trigger words; I automatically asked myself, *"Was that for me."* Then, I sat in my car after services in anger because I could see Parisa clapping as if God were validating her message to me through our Pastor. Although my Pastors told me the letter wasn't of God. I was still experiencing paranoia. I didn't want to be in the same church with her. It was difficult for me, but I pushed through for a while. Yet, her claps and "Amen" seemed isolated in the sanctuary. I decided to take a step back from the church because I couldn't look past the distraction of her being there and wondering if the messages were about me. It sucked. I had no peace and couldn't tell why.

4. INSIDE JOB

I tried to throw a pity party. I asked myself all types of questions. *Why was I being treated like this? How did I end up around people who want to control me by tearing me down with scripture? Most importantly, why do they have so much power?* With tears in my eyes, I heard clear as day, *"Who do you trust, me or them? "Who do I say you are?"* I knew God was flooding me with those questions. After I cried all the tears I could, God asked, *"Are you ready?"* I can't explain how, but I knew *"Are you ready?"* meant surrender. I didn't know where my yes was going to take me, but that day, I yielded to the most painful, yet amazing inside job.

INSIDE JOB # 1

I didn't trust God, and His words were not truly hidden in my heart (Psalm 119:11). I fooled myself into believing that I obeyed the only true God who I professed to love. I attended church, felt good, went to the altar for prayer, and had a lot of "aha" moments. However, those experiences were short lived because I didn't take the time to truly digest and apply what I learned. I ignored that I wasn't giving God one hundred percent. I had to stop treating God like a microwave that I could turn on when I needed to warm up. My worship and intimacy with God were shallow. My faith had no depth. This realization hurt so much, but it was what I needed to know. "That's conviction." There was a soft, loving voice that I began to realize was the Holy Spirit. I knew what condemnation felt like, but I needed to know what God's conviction felt like. It hurt but it was the needed catalyst for change. When my prayers changed from *what's wrong with me* to *God continue to mold and shape me*, I knew the inside job was working.

INSIDE JOB #2

The truth was I struggle with discipline, I can be rebellious, I can be stubborn, I can be prideful, and the list goes on, but by the grace of God, He forgives me and helps me to get it right. Jesus said that He came for those who needed Him, the individuals who were sick (Matthew 9:12, 13). In my case, my weakness was a daily reminder of my need for Jesus. I could no longer let people who couldn't handle who I was make me feel that I wasn't worthy of God's mercy.

I fully understand that God's grace and mercy does not give me the license to stay where I am, but He never wants me to feel condemned. A person can see your weaknesses and couple it with their perception of you and create their reality. Ultimately, some truth with a lot of poison will still kill you. I let the opinion of others put me in a place of bondage. In hindsight, I didn't heed what I told Parisa. God's voice (the scriptures) wasn't the loudest in my ear. The truth was there was no need for me to feel bound or condemned because Jesus came to set the oppressed free and release those who were captive. God challenged me to not just read those words on paper but to trust and genuinely believe that I am one of those people that He came to set free. Don't get me wrong; I understand accountability. It's important to be surrounded with those who want God's best for me. Once I understood that, I knew everyone couldn't be my friend. I developed boundaries to safeguard my heart and mind. I also worked on respecting the boundaries that others set.

INSIDE JOB #3

Forgiveness. I thought I understood what it meant to forgive, but I didn't. You see, I had an "out of sight, out of mind" mentality almost all my life. If you hurt me, the farther away I am from you, the easier it is to move on. This time around, I had to acknowledge my avoidance issue and the bitterness in my heart. I didn't care if that person lived or died. Yeah, that's harsh, but it was my truth. God showed me that it's so much easier for me to forgive those I want to keep close but care less about those I felt were unforgivable. Honestly, I wasn't too far removed from what hurt me. I hurt people as well. I had to remember those times I was self-righteous and started shutting people out of my life in the "name of God." I thought it was a selfless act. In my mind, I was picking God over friends and family. I had to shift my perspective.

The Bible tells us to treat others as we want to be treated, and that love covers all offense. I wasn't operating in love. I already knew what I had to do. I had to forgive quickly. When we ask God to forgive us, it's immediate. He doesn't even think about it anymore. Every time I thought about what Pastor Dev did to me, all types of emotions would rise. I questioned whether I had truly forgiven him. Truth is forgiveness doesn't exempt you from feeling pain. It takes time, so I had to be patient with myself.

INSIDE JOB #4

I was reading my Bible for knowledge, not for living. I had this idea that I didn't know enough, so I started reading the Bible and all books relating to the Bible with the wrong lens. I wanted to stand up for myself. It got to a point where everything seemed like information overload. I followed all the social media teachers, preachers, and motivational speakers but nothing changed. I started going through a mental anguish of comparison and wondered whether I really was getting truth. I had to go back to the basics, and simply give myself to Jesus. I learned about the supernatural miracles, signs, and wonders, but I couldn't effectively lead anyone to Christ. My perspective had to change. I had to believe that God's Word is truly the living word. I shut down all voices (social media), stopped reading for knowledge, and started reading my Bible to live. Scripture in context became my arsenal to navigate life.

Then, I had to do a difficult task. Every thought or word spoken to me or over me had to go through this process: trigger, scripture, introspection, and lesson. The steps involved writing down any thought that triggered a negative emotion, asking myself why (introspection), finding a scripture(s) in context to help me, and finally, asking myself what lesson God was teaching me. Below is what the process looked like:

Trigger: Pastor Dev: "*Nothing you do will prosper. Even if you ever get married, your marriage will fail, your husband will divorce you.*

Parisa: "[Y]*you're making [your future husband] wait. ... Not only are you reaching your mid-30s, ... You're making him wait longer ... because you chose not to get it together, obey God (write the book, love me, etc.), and be developed (in the areas listed in this prophetic word). ... you don't know how to love. You don't know how to be a true friend. ... Your friendships are dysfunctional.*"

Introspection: fear of staying single, lack of confidence, no contentment, lonely, scared, seeking validation, lack of identity

Scriptures:
    I am complete in him, Colossians 2:10
    I am not condemned, Romans 8:1-2
    I am loved eternally, 1 Peter 1:5
    I am kept from falling, Jude 1:24
    I am free forever from sin's power, Romans 6:14
    I follow God's voice, John 10:5
    I guard my heart, Proverbs 4:23
    I draw near to God, James 4:8
    I am not fearful, 2 Timothy 1:7
    God's plan for me is perfect, Jeremiah 29:11
    God's timing is perfect, Ecclesiastes 3:11

SPIRITUALLY ABUSED AND BROKEN

Lesson: Whose voice are you following? Your past actions don't define who you are. Are you striving to walk in love now? (Yes). Do you know that you are complete in me? (Trying to get there). You've been married; remember the times you both laid next to each other feeling lonely? If you're not content in me, you won't be content with the person I bring you. Have I given you a spirit of fear? (No.) So, I need you to walk with boldness. You have the Holy Spirit who's here to help. Ask Him and let Him work. Guard your heart; people will always have opinions and feel a certain way about you. Continue with me daily. I will search your heart and remove anything that's not like Me. What I have for you is perfect; I won't keep anything good from you. It's all in my timing so worrying about who I have for you won't get you there faster. Trust the process. Your only concern is to do My will. Stop worrying about what people have to say about you. No one can take or give life except me. You can be here today and gone tomorrow. So, cast down those thoughts and be about My business. You're in a fight; My word is the weapon. Continue to do this and see how I strengthen and mature you. Don't' waste time trying to prove to others that they are wrong; spend time knowing truth that can only be found in knowing Me.

The inside job can be a book on its own. Your healing journey might not look like mine, but ultimately, with God, it's possible. He's got you. I'm just in awe of God's healing power. He took me through what I call Holy Spirit Therapy and continues to do so. I shed so many tears and experienced so much joy in this process. Changing my thoughts and replacing the voice of others is a daily habit. Do I always get it right? No. Some days, I don't want to fight my thoughts and let life get the best of me. Still, I start over again the next day. God's mercy is new every day. The good and the bad are a journey to exactly where God wants me to be. The level of control a person has on my life is dependent on what I give that person. I can no longer question how and why I put myself through the abuse. I find comfort in knowing that everything I've gone through in my 34 years of life isn't news to God. His plan is perfect. This Christian walk is not easy but walking this life out with God is so much better than trying to figure it out on my own.

PART III
AWARENESS

1. CAN YOU RELATE?

Are you reading this book and realizing that you may be in a church that's spiritually abusive or controlling? If your answer is yes, don't delay getting as far away from that person or group of people. Don't dismiss what you feel on the account of uncertainty. I understand not everyone's situation will look the same. Some are more dangerous than others. In hindsight, I handled properly some things and should have done others differently for my safety. First, once I realized what type of situation I was in, I shared it with another person in the same situation. That was the first mistake you don't want to make. In most cases, you're taught to refute anything someone says about the leader or church. However, you must focus on saving yourself.

Most abusive leaders are proactive. If they know ahead of time that you are thinking about leaving, they will try to manipulate you into staying. For example, when I mentioned I thought it was time to leave, Pastor Dev used scare tactics by telling me that I would be cursed and fail at everything. Unfortunately, I was not strong enough at the time to stand up for myself. So, it's best not to show any signs of doubt around the abusive leader. Once you've established it's time to go, reach out to people outside of the inner circle. In some cases, you might be in a situation where you've been isolated so that may be difficult. Whomever you can get to, make sure the person is not affiliated with the abusive leader in any way. I was connected to the church's academy center as the lead director. One mistake I made was trying to remove myself from their business before I left. If there is any way to remove yourself without being present, do so. The goal is to get away from the abusive leader.

As difficult as it may be, you also must cut off communication with those individuals still connected to the leader because they are still under the abuser's control, so whatever that abuser says will be the final say so. If there must be any communication, find someone who can deal with the abuser without being affected; it can be a family member, friend, or coworker. For example, when I left, I had two cousins take items that were being stored at my house to the cult. Once I walked out those doors, I didn't talk to that Pastor again. Remember, you are in a vulnerable state, so hearing negativity from the leader or anyone connected won't help you get out or start your healing process. For that individual who can't think of anyone who can help, the most important thing is safety. Some people may try to minimize what you're going through, but don't be afraid to utilize resources such as crisis hotlines. If you must, get the police involved because it may be your only way out. Don't underestimate an abuser. The leader I was under had a gun. I moved out of my apartment a few weeks after leaving the church, I didn't feel safe with them knowing where I lived. Abuse in any form is dangerous. Safety first!

Every form of abuse is ultimately about control. It's easy to beat yourself up. I remember feeling worthless. I told myself that I stayed in the cult for so long because I was a liar, manipulator, selfish, and a gossiper. I let my actions become my identity and could only focus on who I wasn't. I couldn't conceptualize that God really loved someone like me. I threw myself a pity party every time I thought about what I went through. I blamed myself and rationalized that no one held me in chains and told me I couldn't leave. Manipulation is a powerful tool; because of it, I felt imprisoned.

We are to acknowledge our imperfections and weakness, but never walk in condemnation. I had to come to the reality that I am an imperfect person, but I serve a perfect God. I also had to accept that not only does God love the abused, He also loves the abuser. Hurt people who don't heal usually hurt those around them. With that knowledge, I knew that forgiveness was key. I couldn't wish anyone harm. I had to get to a place where I prayed for them. I'm not saying it's an easy thing to do, but with God and time, the feelings of anger and bitterness will go away. I wanted God to change my heart. Overtime, my pain turned into prayers that God would turn Pastor Dev's heart. I also prayed that he would be exposed so that others wouldn't continue to get hurt. I realize that I am that voice and so are you. Don't be afraid to share your story. I know it doesn't happen right away, but change doesn't come without truth.

I walked out of that situation feeling that I couldn't be me again. Don't let shame cripple you. The healing process looks different for each person. Get the help that you need. I had difficultly navigating my thoughts and emotions. Speaking to a professional helped me put everything into perspective as well. Your story might be ugly in your eyes but ask God to show you His view because all things work together for our good (Romans

8:28). Remember, we're not promised that we won't experience trials and tribulations in this life. There's one thing for sure, God will never leave you nor forsake you. Healing takes time. I still find myself refuting the negative words spoken to me. I'm learning to love me again. I had to stop beating myself up and realize the abuse didn't happen in one day, nor will the healing occur overnight. I'm healing from three years of spiritual abuse as well as verbal and emotional abuse. Process your pain, but don't dwell in it. Get help, surround yourself with a supportive community, and let God work.

When you're in the phase of knowing God for yourself, be careful what you share with others. The last thing you want is someone to run with the thoughts that you are unclear about. The "but God said" people can cause you to relapse into all sorts of negative emotions. Feelings of condemnation, guilt, and unworthiness are just a few that rise. Remember, at one point, an abuser defined your relationship with God. Think about a dating relationship or platonic relationship. The getting to know each other phase is typically fun, but if you had a bad experience prior, you'll struggle, make mistakes, and even question if the relationship will last. Your journey with God may mirror this process after spiritual abuse. Your faith feels challenged.

It may seem ironic, but God is the only one who can help you with your faith. You may wonder how to trust the God you're struggling to know; it requires faith. Ultimately, freedom is in truth, and truth is the Word of God. Jesus said, "I am the way, the truth, and the life and no one comes to the father except through me (John 14:6)." All the words that Jesus spoke can be

SPIRITUALLY ABUSED AND BROKEN

found in the Bible. In there, Jesus said He only did what his father told him to do and that outside of him he could do nothing (John 5:19). Once you start reading the Bible for yourself and listening to the words of God, the faith will come (Romans 10:17).

2. FRIENDS AND FAMILY

The one thing I heard the most from those who love me was no one knew how to tell me something was wrong. Some were afraid of hurting me because of how happy and involved I was when I first joined the cult. Remember, the abuser is proactive while loved ones tend to be reactive. More than likely, the leader has prepared those around him or her for what to expect. For example, if someone said I spent too much time in church, Pastor Dev said that people wouldn't understand the work I was doing for God. He told me to lie about my whereabouts, avoid their call, or tell them we were at work. Don't take what your loved one is doing personally; instead, be there for them. Don't respond with negativity or show anger. Even when you can tell they have isolated themselves, try to keep an open line of communication. My friend Diana knew something was wrong even though she didn't have specific details, so she continued to check on me despite me never reaching out to her. She remained consistent and always let me talk and share what was on my mind. Be that person. If possible, learn as much as you can about the leader so that you know what you are up against. Here is a snippet of what Diana thought.

SPIRITUALLY ABUSED AND BROKEN

"When I first heard you talk about the [church], my stomach turned. I had a very uneasy feeling, and for some odd reason, I thought I was being very judgmental because a weird feeling came over me when you told me that the Pastor was from India. I love all people, so it bothered me that I felt weird about that detail. The Pastor telling you that wearing braids was basically a sin and giving you the okay to tell a lie in order to cover up a conversation that he had with you about another member was very weird for me. When you told me that he would tell [you] personal things about the other members, I was bothered, but something told me that I would probably never hear from you again if I mentioned any of these feelings. You spoke a lot about his advice, but I often felt that he quoted scriptures to support his lies or used scriptures to manipulate you. I didn't find anything interesting about the organization, and I made it up in my mind that I wouldn't visit even if you asked me to visit. This also bothered [me] because I never met the leader of the organization, but I had a very strong opinion of him."

Despite what she felt, Diana stayed supportive, and at my lowest point, I trusted her enough to listen to the video she sent me. So, don't shut your loved one out. It's difficult, but keep in mind that they are being controlled and not thinking clearly. Today, Diana is still part of my support system. She is available to me whenever I need her. She also gives me genuine tough love when necessary.

On the other hand, my family was initially reactive. I randomly popped up at family functions. As time passed, they rarely saw me. I can't blame them, but they stopped communicating with me. Isolation was so powerful that, in my time of need, I completely forgot how many people I could call on. All my siblings lived in different states; for all they knew, I was always busy doing something in church. Like Diana, one of my cousins didn't give up on me. She always checked on me and continued to reach out regularly. She was also hurt when I isolated myself, but she realized a bigger issue was at hand. This is what she had to say:

> "First, Ima say that I was excited that you were into church. You were into church, but it was just something weird. It was a weird feeling like why couldn't we see you. Why couldn't you interact with people? It's like you don't have a moment to breathe. That Pastor was sucking the life out of you. It was horrible to see you this way. You didn't open up to me. I could tell that you weren't happy after a while. You were telling us how hard you were working, but I no longer saw the joy in you. The family get togethers just ended. We were tired of you sneaking in and out rushing to church. That Pastor was sucking you dry. I didn't know what to say."

I never knew my family felt this way. If I did, I probably would have pushed further away from them, thinking they were not being supportive of my involvement with church. My cousin consistently reached out to me and picked me up the day I walked away from the cult. All further communication with Pastor Dev went through her. I didn't know much of what was said because she protected me and only shared with me what I needed to know. Build a positive support system. You never know the moment you'll be needed to help your loved one get away from the abuser.

Also, remain hopeful. If there is a way to get the person out of the control of the abuser, do so, but make sure that your loved one is no longer controlled by the leader because that only pushes him or her away from you and closer to the them. When your loved one is away from the abuser, make sure the focus is not on you but on them getting help. I couldn't have handled what anyone else had to say until I was healed. So, make sure that your loved one is ready to hear how you felt because you don't want him or her to feel guilty. The goal is to be supportive and believe the absolute best.

3. DON'T BE DECEIVED

The same Bible that was used to control me is also the book that warns us about deceptive leaders. Spiritual abuse can come from anyone. The Bible warns us to be careful of those who come to deceive. Jesus taught His disciples to beware of false prophets who come in sheep's clothing but inwardly are ravenous wolves (Matthew 7:15). He also said that false prophets will lead many astray (Matthew 24:11) and we are to be wise as a serpent and innocent as a dove (Matthew 10:16). These false prophets are religious imposters.

The abuser, like a ravenous wolf, preys on the vulnerable. Vulnerability looked like me in part one of this book. I trusted Pastor Dev and his wife to counsel me concerning my issues of rejection, abandonment, guilt, and so on. Initially, I thought he helped by encouraging me, but when it was convenient, my past became a tool of control and manipulation. In the book of 2 Timothy, the Apostle Paul warned Timothy that there were people among him who would creep into households and capture weak women who were burdened with sins and led astray by various passions, always learning and never able to arrive at a knowledge of truth. Like these women, I thought I was learning, but I wasn't getting truth. I was learning to conform to whatever my leader said. If Pastor Dev said it was okay to steal, I did it.

If he said it was okay to lie to my family about my whereabouts, I did it. Whoever causes one of God's children to sin, it's better they take a great millstone, tie it around their neck, and drown in the depths of the sea (Matthew 18:6). Figuratively and literally, that's a heavy weight to carry. The signs may not be visible at first but remain watchful.

A person can only put on a mask for so long. Jesus said that you'll recognize them by their fruits (Matthew 7:16). In other words, pay attention to people's actions, the words they speak, and their interactions with those close to them, especially family. "Behold, I am sending you out as sheep in the midst of wolves, so be wise as serpents and innocent as doves (Matthew 10:16). We can apply this same principle that Jesus taught his disciples to be wise by understanding the cunning ways of abusers (snakes), but make sure to remain pure and guilt free (innocent as a dove) from their actions so that you can rightfully judge the person. When you are living in sin, it is difficult to see it in someone else. That's the whole point; if an abuser can keep you in a place of condemnation, you'll never feel bold enough to call the abuser out.

I asked myself, *how can someone who knows nothing about church or has never read a Bible avoid church cults and spiritually abusive people? What happens to the person whose first introduction into a church community is abusive and controlling?* The Bible says that nothing is hidden except to be made manifest; nor is anything secret except to come to light (Mark 4:22). If anyone has ears to hear, let him hear (Mark 4:23). God doesn't want us to be in the dark. Throughout the Bible, He warns that deception is all around us. We must share Jesus Christ with those who don't know him. We need to shed light on leaders who try to control people and teach those around us to understand the Word of God. Ultimately, spreading the gospel and discipleship are key.

I was afraid of being open about what I went through, but my story is proof of God's power. The Gospel of Jesus Christ is what healed me. In what I called my broken state, nothing I went through could separate me from the love of Jesus Christ. I'm confident in Christ because of the Gospel. We can't be ashamed of sharing who He is. Most importantly, we should help others understand the Word of God. Jesus told the Pharisees and Sadducees that they were wrong because they didn't know scripture or the power of God, but they presented themselves as Godly. Today, people are being hurt and turned away from God through deception and control.

We are responsible for what we know. Don't think your story can't help someone. I know my story is no longer for me. It's to help someone else who may be experiencing the same thing I went through. We overcome by the blood of the lamb, Jesus Christ, and the power of our testimony (Rev 12:11). To help those who have not yet experienced true freedom in Christ, we must line up our actions with the Word of God and rightly teach truth. A person in chains can't set anyone free. In other words, I couldn't help anyone being bound myself. There's no comparison to the freedom that only God can give. Let's get free and stay free!

4. Q&A

I asked a few of my closest friends, family, and coworkers questions that would give me perspective of what it looked like to be on the outside looking in. Despite the different relational dynamics, notice the similar thoughts that most of my friends and family had.

1. **When you first heard me talk about [the church], what did you think? What sounded weird? What was interesting?**

    - *"No red flags were raised initially. You seemed happy and upbeat about the church and the messages the minister was delivering." ~ Danielle*

    - *"I was initially happy for Sandra for finding a church home where she was involved, a leader, and was able to use her strength to develop programs that benefited the church. What sounded weird was how she felt like she needed to isolate herself (which was the message from the Shepard of the church) from the people who loved her and who truly had her best interest at heart. I didn't see anything that was interesting but what I thought was unique was the diverse people who attended the church." ~ Hakemia*

- *"When I first heard you talk about [the church], I was excited for you because I knew it was important that you find a church home where you can connect. I thought that there were several opportunities for growth and that you would be able to work on getting your licensure for childcare (although, I had never heard you discuss this interest prior). I thought it may have been a new-found love and this was the perfect opportunity to serve the Lord and work with children. Initially, there weren't any red flags to me." ~Jessica*

2. What where your thoughts about the church when you visited? How did you feel being there? What did you think about the people?

- *"I didn't like the church. It felt heavy. Like it was anchored by something. I did not like the people. I felt like they all had motives." ~ Leondra*

- *"It felt like a family-oriented place honestly. I just didn't like how pastor treated the guy who did surround sound." ~ Nerlande*

3. What changes did you begin to see in me?

- *"You withdrew. I also felt like you were following the crowd." ~ Leondra*

- *"You were disciplined in the word, but I felt scared to say things to you bc I thought you were going to PREACH to me." ~ Nerlande*

- *"As time went on, you were very withdrawn from social settings that had previously been a normal part of your life. Our friendship circle (from Upward Bound days) was always missing you at gatherings. We did not communicate often by phone, text, and certainly not in person. You literally seemed to do ALL things for the church and be consumed by the church's events and other happenings." ~ Danielle*

- *"She isolated herself. She worked constantly on initiatives that the pastor wanted her to rather than it truly being God's will. To me, I seen it as spiritual manipulation." ~Hakemia*

- *"You were more into "church" than the word of God." ~Carline*

- *"This is hard to say because you're my girl and I love you. However, I started to see you walking down a path that was unpleasant for me to watch. You would be up until 5am on a Wednesday morning because you were at Bible Study all night and then drag to work Thursday. I used to*

think to myself that this pastor has no respect for people's time and was taking advantage of you. I knew then that it was a cult. You only involved yourself with church and there was no balance. I felt I couldn't talk to you anymore and open up and just be myself because I would either get a "Word" or be condemned. I was afraid that somehow you would cut me off because I didn't fit into your world of "holier than thou." You were always at church, running errands for the church, doing church related stuff at work (which, let's face it, we all do but yours was overboard), doing door to door and mall outreach, etc. I knew that something had to be up because it was an "us 4 and no more mentality" and I felt like you were being secluded."
~ Jessica

4. How did me being at that church affect our relationship?

- *"It didn't. You Sandy Pandy. I prayed about it and dismissed my feelings. I thought that maybe I was jealous because God was calling you for higher service and I was still waiting on the phone to ring lol"* ~ Leondra

- *"We did not communicate as often as we had for so many years. When we did talk, the conversation flowed well, but there was always a mention of the fact that you were tied up in church stuff and not getting home until 2, 3, and 4 a.m."* ~ Danielle

- *"She was my backbone and best friend prior to joining the church, but overtime, our relationship dwindled. We didn't speak much over a 3-year period."* ~Hakemia

- *"I felt our relationship was, in a nutshell, non-existent. When we were both in the office, we had conversations, but they were very surface and, you know, I am not a surface chick. That realness and rawness was gone. I used to be upset about what you told me about your relationship changing with your friend, which you're the Godmother of her daughter. I felt that if I was not supportive of your church, then I would lose you as a friend so I remained silent, but it seemed as though everyone was cut off because you were busy doing things for what seemed to be the "Glory of God," but we all could see that something was definitely wrong. You can be all about church and your relationship with Christ and still maintain healthy relationships with everyone (unless detrimental to your walk)."* – Jessica

5. Did you experience any hurt by my previous affiliation with that organization?

- *"No... Not by what you did but because of what I did. God spoke to me about that church. I felt like I was supposed to share it, and I didn't because I felt like you wouldn't take it from me because I'm not super churchy. I think sometimes when we are searching for belonging and acknowledgement, we can be taken advantage of. Being different is lonely, especially when you are called and anointed"* ~ Leondra

- *"I cannot say that I experienced hurt, but concern. You were missed.... the fun, crazy, impulsive gal that I had grown to love as like a sister from another mister was no longer that. There were times when those in our inner circle would discuss you and your involvement in the church and how strange it was that you were ALWAYS doing church business. We often discussed that it was cult-like behavior. However, I refrained from discussing this with you as a friend because I did not want you to feel as if I was attacking your walk with God. I also felt that perhaps you had reached a level in your relationship with God that I, who was not nearly as involved in church happenings as you were, had not reached and could not understand or relate to."* ~Danielle

- *"Yes, offended because she felt as though her spiritual literacy was more advance than I assume because of her involvement at the church."* ~Hakemia

- *"I honestly thought you was going to cut me off at some point. If pastor said something about me."* ~ Nerlande

- *"Yes. I really consider you a great friend, and you have been there for me during my growing stages. I was hurt when I invited you to performances and events that I had at my church and you did not attend. I didn't feel supported. Also,*

I was mostly hurt when you didn't attend my wedding, but at that point, I understood that you most likely wouldn't have come. More so, I felt hurt that a church (which is a positive thing) could change our relationship in a negative way. My heart hurt the day you and I had a long phone conversation regarding what you were actually going through at the church and the abuse, but I was relieved that you decided to stop attending. It still bothers me that you endured that. I don't have any more thoughts other than you know I love you, and I am so happy for you that you have gotten through this and still coming out on top! I back you 110%."
~ Jessica

ACKNOWLEDGEMENTS

To My Abba Father, I give you all the glory and honor. Without you I am nothing!

To my brothers and sisters, Walner Leandre, Snayder Leandre, Renus Leandre, Enide Milord, Elta Cetoute, and Carline Pierre. Thank you for being my forever friends. I love you! I thank God that I can do life with you all.

To my soul sister and friend, Dominique Devereaux Johnson thank you for your obedience. Who knows where I would be if you didn't say yes to God. I love you to Life!

To my family and friends who didn't give up on me. Thank you for being present. Your wisdom and encouragement bless my life every day.